I LAUGH . . .
I CRY . . .

CONFESSIONS OF A PASTOR

Don Paulk

KINGDOM
PUBLISHERS

P.O. Box 7300 • Atlanta, GA 30357

To Joan
my baby sister
with whom I laughed and cried . . .

Acknowledgements

There are many people who play important roles in my life. A few have taken the time to help me accomplish something creative. I would like to thank each one of them for the help they provided.

The members of my family have been a constant source of help to me. My wife, Clariece, provided not only technical assistance, but her love and patience have been my salvation. LaDonna, my daughter, has been my joy since the day she was born. Now her assistance in my work is invaluable. My son, Donnie Earl, is a constant source of inspiration and joy. Deanna and Dana, my niece and nephew, have brought an additional measure of joy and assistance since becoming a part of our household.

A special thanks to my brother, Bishop Earl Paulk, who has given me the opportunity to develop this book and begin to satisfy my desire to write. I am also grateful for the prayerful support of the entire Chapel Hill Presbytery.

A note of thanks to Sharalee Lucas who was instrumental in causing me to put this book together and spent many hours working to see that the dream became a reality. I also thank Don Ross whose expertise and talents helped make the book attractive. A special thanks to Donna Eubanks, who not only typeset the book, but worked many overtime hours in putting all the loose ends together.

I also wish to thank the editors who worked so hard in taking my thoughts and transforming them into something readable. I especially thank Tricia Weeks, whose work demonstrated her love for the ministry. Also, Gayle Blackwood, Chris Oborne and Janis McFarland helped make sure the book was not only enjoyable for me to write, but for you to read . . .

FOREWORD
by Jamie Buckingham

Here's the book you've been waiting for. The sub-title could be: *Everything You've Always Wanted to Know About Pastors, But Were Afraid to Ask.* Well, almost everything.

We've all suspected, despite their diligent efforts to conceal it, that pastors are people too. Granted, a lot of them seem to go out of their way to convince us otherwise. But deep down inside most of us have thought that if we stripped away all their vestments, took off their collars, snatched the microphone (spit and all) out of their hands, and forbade them to use words and phrases like "brethren," "yonder," "It was good to fellowship with you," and "Weeeelll, HallelUUUUUUUUUUjah!" we would discover they're just like the rest of us. Plain old people.

Don Paulk is plain people. Now during the day he looks like a pastor. In fact, he looks like a priest—and that's two steps beyond pastor on the Accepted Liturgical Scale (ALS).

The ALS, which is graded on a scale of 1-10, is as follows:

(1) Plain old ordinary pew-sitting, hymn-singing, money-giving, hard working church member.

(2) Sunday school teacher. (There are ranks inside the Sunday school teacher category. Nursery worker is at the bottom because everyone knows all they do is babysit. Youth workers are next to bottom because they never seem to last very long and most of them wind up fleeing into the desert where they rip their clothes and beat their heads on rocks. Adult teachers are at the top, but they are ranked, too, depending on how large a class they teach and how wealthy and famous their class members are. For instance, a class which contains the mayor, an assistant to the governor, or a wealthy widow ranks higher than a class of Yuppies or dump truck drivers.)

(3) Church staff members. (All staff members except church secretaries are included on this level. Secretaries rate

even less than church members unless she is the pastor's personal secretary who is rated equal with an archbishop.)
(4) Pastors.
(5) Missionaries. (Some people rank missionaries number 10, while others don't rank them at all. I've given them a number 5 to please both camps.)
(6) Priests. (All kinds, even those who drink beverages with little olives and onions in the bottom of the glass.)
(7) Seminary professors. (Unless you teach religious education or music, which drops you down to a number 3.)
(8) Bishops.
(9) Archbishops.
(10) Popes. (Some Pentecostal groups substitute apostles for popes. Nearly all TV evangelists put themselves at this rank.)

Thus, on the ALS, Don Paulk rates a 4. However, those in his congregation suspect that even though he looks like a number 6 he is really a number 1 in disguise. Just plain people.

This book proves it. He laughs and cries—just like plain people. And he doesn't do it in King James English. In fact, the book will make you laugh and cry, also. It will do something else; it will show you the ALS is really upside down. In other words, the greatest is the least. That means even though Don ranks himself as a number 1, by Kingdom standards he rates a number 10.

Contents

I LAUGH . . .
I CRY . . .

I sat in a chair at the monastery and looked at the crucifix on the wall. My eyes trailed about the small room, comfortable but not ostentatious. It was a room prepared especially for men of the cloth who sought a place to be alone with their thoughts and perhaps find answers to questions in their lives or rediscover the direction that had somehow become obscured. I was not Catholic, yet I felt a divine presence there.

I was seeking answers. I wanted to know what meaning my life really had. I tried mentally to prepare a ledger of plusses and minuses in my life. As I reflected, I realized I had so many things for which to be grateful. Among the outstanding things that came to mind immediately were two attractive, healthy children. I had a beautiful, talented wife whose heart

was totally involved in the ministry. I had good
health. I had friends who loved me and whom I loved
dearly. Yet, something was missing. Strange . . . here
I was a pastor who should know happiness in life.
What was the missing ingredient?

I had been in the ministry for over twenty years.
Perhaps I was a different type of minister from what
many consider "a preacher" to be. In the first place, I
don't do a lot of preaching. My brother, Earl Paulk,
Jr., does most of that.

When we founded the church in 1960, Earl had
already been preaching for a number of years and I
was fresh out of college. We evaluated our talents and
agreed to do whatever best suited the ministry. Earl
could preach, so he would do that. My wife, Clariece,
who has few peers in sacred music, was a natural in
that area. As for me, I realized there were many ways
to minister in addition to preaching. I found expression in youth work, recreation, directing the choir,
teaching, visiting, community and civic involvement
as well as necessary chores such as driving the
church bus, operating audio equipment and oversee-
ing church maintenance. But still, what was that one
element of ministry that could bring a sense of fulfill-
ment that seemed to elude me?

Eventually we grew large enough to begin a
church bulletin, so I assumed the editorship. Even

though I had always enjoyed writing, this was really my first serious journalistic attempt beyond term papers in school. Whatever "talent" I may have in writing was either accidental or a God-given ability. I choose to think of it as a divine gift. I was a Christian Education major in college. Unfortunately, I was more interested in athletics and a social life in college than academics. I graduated knowing how to thread a 16 millimeter projector and little else!

In writing our little newsletter, I realized I had finally discovered a form of ministry that I really enjoyed. Perhaps, this was the missing ingredient!

As I sat staring at the crucifix on the wall of that little cubicle in the monastery, I realized my ministry was unique. Even though speaking from a pulpit would continue to be a part of my overall ministry, I knew the single most important gift God had given me in ministry was the ability to communicate through words. Sensitivity to people and their emotions is an integral part of that gift. I must translate to the page what exists in the mind, the memory and the soul.

I returned home from the monastery with a new mission . . . to write books some day; not just religious books that espouse doctrine and theology, but books that are touchpoints for our very lives; books to bring not only information, but inspiration.

Through the years, writing has become my first ministerial love. It is a catharsis for me at times. At other times, writing provides a place for emotional release, and perhaps even a way to vent my frustrations.

But hopefully, it also is a medium for expressing joy and happiness. I seek to amuse and entertain, while at the same time challenge and inspire. I want to say things to people without making them feel they are being "preached at!"

Aside from standard English courses, I had no formal training in journalism. I only knew that I was able to communicate with people through writing. I still dangle participles and split infinitives occasionally and it takes several proofreaders to make sure that I keep my tenses correct!

I'm not very sure when or where, for I don't remember dates well, but one day I read something by a Christian writer named Jamie Buckingham. His words were a revelation to me! I never thought someone could write with his style and still be considered a Christian, much less a preacher! Here was a man who wrote what he thought, not just theological jargon expected from a staid preacher. He dared to challenge people's minds. He asked questions that I had never seen in print, but had privately asked myself many times. It opened a whole new vista in writing for me. I didn't pattern my writing style after his, but it surely did give me a new sense of freedom. Finally, I could write things I felt, ask questions that were in my mind and say things that needed to be said—even if it sounded irreverent, and in some cases, heretical!

As our church grew, so did our publications. I started a newspaper called *Harvest Time*. I chose the newspaper format because our society is geared toward it as an acceptable vehicle for news. I wanted the publication to be totally believable. I had seen so many religious periodicals that emphasized sensationalism and exaggeration. They were merely spiritual "hype" that few people believed. Such irresponsible journalism serves only to make the Church a laughingstock before the world. I purposed to create a newspaper that had credibility in religious circles. When people read it, I wanted them to accept it as believable. Hopefully, it has accomplished that. *Harvest Time* has been renamed *Thy Kingdom Come*, and has grown to a circulation of about 40,000 readers, serving as a major outreach tool for our church.

One of the regular features of the paper has been a column I write. I have received many favorable comments from readers. However, I suppose it is fair to admit that not everyone appreciates my brand of journalism!

I write about things that interest and amuse me.

I often write about my family. They definitely interest and amuse me! I like animals and so I write about them. I write about feelings . . .

I am often asked why I haven't written a book. When asked this question, I have a fairly standard set of replies: First, I explain that the world doesn't need another book to clutter our shelf space. It seems that every book that has anything to say about any issue has already been written by someone . . . somewhere!

Secondly, I explain that the name Don Paulk isn't exactly a household word. I have a moderate recognition factor among members of my church, a few people in southwest Dekalb County, and even some of my family members, particularly my immediate family! So, any book I might write would be welcomed only by those aforementioned, plus a few close friends. The rest of the world would probably respond with a great yawn!

And finally, books should be written only if they are worthy of their existence. Either they should answer life's great questions, or address some pertinent issues of the day. I tell them that I intend to write a book when the time is right and there is a need for it. Hopefully, the time is right and there exists a need.

As I thought about it, I realized a great need exists in all of us . . . a need to laugh and a need to cry. When we can do neither, we become mere robots, stoically going through mundane lives feeling indifference to pain or pleasure.

After being a pastor for twenty-six years, I have had my share of laughter and tears. I have been able to laugh with those who rejoiced, and have wept bitter tears with those who suffered tragedy or despair.

This book is a compilation of some of the most notable columns I have written over the years. The publication date is noted with each chapter. In the beginning, none of these columns were written for further publication. Most of them were written in a few minutes in order to beat deadlines! But I loved doing it! In many ways, writing has become my "pulpit."

As I pulled out past issues of *Harvest Time* and reread my columns, I experienced many emotions. I relived some joyful occasions, and also suffered through old pains again. But I love nostalgia. I enjoyed the sentimental journeys I took into the past . . .

Perhaps some of my thoughts may seem irreverent to readers, but please don't judge too quickly. Catch the spirit in which the words were written . . . by a pastor who has experienced all the emotions shared by the brotherhood of man. Hopefully, I can share some of these emotions with you.

If reading this book points out humor in life and brings you laughter, I will laugh with you. And if you find something poignant or even sad which moves you to tears, I will understand, for I cried when I wrote it. I love to meet people who are able to read things and be moved to tears or laughter . . . they are indeed my soul mates!

As you read this book, you will discover that I, too, am very much like you. And, I confess to you, I laugh . . . I cry . . .

1

IN AND OUT OF AFRICA
– April 1983 –

Pastor Don in Benin City, Nigeria

Clariece's folded hands

The nose of the jumbo jet lifted skyward as the surge of its powerful engines quickly whisked us into the clouds. I was off to see the world . . . and I mean the REST of the world!

I had traveled some. Daddy was a traveling preacher. Before I started to school I had passed through all 48 contiguous United States plus Mexico and Canada. Admittedly, I was probably sleeping when I visited many of them!

During my adult life I had visited various other places, none of which, however, had prepared me sufficiently for this trip to Nigeria. For those of you who missed that day in geography class, Nigeria is deep in the heart of Africa. Now, the big Pan Am jet was hurtling me toward the dark continent that before today had only been pictures I had seen in

National Geographic.

When we left New York, it was a damp and cold day with the temperature in the low forties. We were dressed appropriately in our woolen suits and top coats, which shortly would be like albatrosses around our necks.

I surveyed the passengers who boarded this international flight. I immediately observed they were a strange breed of people! I felt as if I had been cast in an old Bogart film with a wide array of international types, complete with the debonair and sinister, the espionage agents and the defectors. But most dreaded of all . . . the TERRORISTS! I looked closely to see if I could detect any bulges under their clothes that might be machine guns!

The flight to Lagos would take all night, so almost everyone settled down into their seats to sleep. Some of the veteran travelers, who obviously had taken this flight before, knew exactly what to do. After everyone had taken their seats and the doors had been shut, these veterans of the airways moved to vacant seats in the huge L10ll and staked out their claims. The armrests could be lifted, providing a fairly good bed. But there was no way I was going to sleep! After all, someone had to help the pilot get our aircraft across the Atlantic Ocean! I volunteered!

I looked about and watched all the potential victims sleeping peacefully. Now I knew how Jesus felt when He surveyed Jerusalem in the Garden of Gethsemane. Why couldn't my traveling companions tarry with me in my travail? Then I wondered if they slept easily because they were more spiritually prepared to face impending doom than I!

Trying to occupy my mind with the voyage, I scrutinized the inside of our plane. Little did I realize how I would long to get back aboard a Pan Am aircraft where English would be the first language explaining how to inflate a life jacket. That would become very important later. I had to listen dumbly through several other languages before they got to the one I understood. When flying over the ocean all night, you definitely think about the importance of inflatable gear designed to save your life! And I didn't care to wade through French, Italian, Swahili and God knows what other dialects to learn which string to pull in an emergency!

I had the feeling that if disaster did strike, I would have ended up strangling myself to death trying to figure out how to inflate my vest. Meanwhile, the flight attendant would calmly instruct all the French passengers how to don their life saving equipment!

In situations like this, I have a tendency to

allow my imagination to run amok! Every air pocket
the plane encountered struck fear to my heart, which
was already in my throat and brought a prayer to my
lips. "God, You know I only came because I was convinced I was doing this for YOUR cause. You KNOW
if I were going to take a vacation, it wouldn't be to
Nigeria! Please don't leave me now. I still have young
children at home who need a father!"

I pressed my face close to the porthole to try to
gain my bearings. Total darkness. Not even a moon to
be seen. I cupped my hands around my eyes to close
out the light. I finally thought I could make out
some distant stars. I tried to see lights on the ground.
Nothing below!

That meant we were still over the open sea. I
tried to calculate how much fuel we had left. Had
they figured it right? Did we have enough to make
land? Were we moving toward the sun or away from
it? Which way does the earth turn, anyway? I silently
berated myself for not listening better in school when
these subjects were explained.

I realized I was becoming emotional. I felt like
crying. I couldn't cry here . . . grown men don't cry
in public. Well, maybe they can if they are having a
spiritual experience. That's it! I would raise my hands
and people would think I was praying!

Just as I was about to stage this spiritual happening, I spotted something starboard . . . or was it portside? I was beginning to feel like a veteran traveler, navigating only by starlight. Yes, there they were . . . lights on the ground. Land ho! We had made it across the ocean. I breathed another prayer in my continuing litany.

I didn't see many lights, but then how many lights can there be in a place called Dakar, Senegal? The only lights that really concerned me, however, were the ones on the runway. Soon I would discover that this was not exactly Hartsfield International Airport!

Their idea of landing lights is a couple of guys with flashlights running up and down the runway waving them wildly and pointing in several directions at once! But through the providence of the Almighty, we did land. I looked out to get my first glimpse of Africa up close. From what I saw, this was as close as I wanted to get! The ground crew squatted on the tops of their World War II vintage jeeps waiting for us to taxi to a stop.

Two guys pushed some steps up to the door of our plane and positioned them. Another guy with a machine gun stationed himself at the foot of the steps. I tried to decide if he was there to keep us on the plane or to keep someone else from boarding . . . or if he just wanted to show off his new Uzi machine gun. I can assure you, I had no desire to find out exactly why he was there! This was my first inkling that guns are very big in Africa. Whoever carries the biggest gun has the most respect! I know he certainly had mine!

After refueling, we were airborne again for our next stop, a place called Monrovia which is in Liberia. It was 4 a.m. by my watch, but I had no idea what time it was where we were. I only knew it was in the middle of the night.

The giant plane soared along on this leg of the trip which was about another 1,000 miles. Soon everyone was comatose again. I had resumed the controls in my own cockpit! Finally, from sheer exhaustion I drifted off in a fitful nap, dreaming of crashing planes and blazing machine guns!

I was stirred back to reality by the bumping of rough air. I resumed my vigil at the window, staring into the black of night searching for lights. Then, faintly on the horizon, a red glow began to emerge. The sun was coming up. I watched the blazing red ball lift slowly into the murky darkness forming a long, iridescent curve that outlined the horizon of the earth. It was breathtaking! Surely a God that created such magnificent beauty would take care of one scared guy somewhere over Africa!

Shortly I felt the plane begin its descent to

earth. By now the sun had fully risen. As we descended, we were totally enveloped in white, filmy clouds. Actually it looked more like thick fog. I could see to the end of the wing and no further. I hoped and prayed the pilot had better vision than I!

Again fear gripped my heart! If they had no better landing instruments at this airport than in Dakar, things could become very scary! I soon learned that here you fly by VR . . . which apparently stands for visual reference. And that means if you can't see, you can't land . . . doesn't it? Well, I guess after you have flown a thousand miles, your lack of fuel pretty much dictates that you WILL land . . . one way or the other!

Let me paint the scenario: They ease down through the fog in what I call a "grope" mode . . . hoping some other craft isn't "groping" in the same vicinity. I could sense the pilot was inching his way down. I was certain that he couldn't see any better than I . . . the only difference was he had a frontal view of the fog and I had a side view!

The pilot had lowered the landing gear long ago. I decided he did this so he could tell when we were at tree top level! When the tires brushed their tips, our intrepid leader would know we were close to terra firma! I was searching desperately for some sign of earth. I only hoped we saw it before it "saw" us!

Suddenly I caught sight of land . . . no, make that waves. WAVES! O my God, why hast Thou forsaken me? My life flashed before my eyes. I remembered sins I had committed as far back as 1943! I saw the faces of people dear to me . . . the faces of my children.

About this time the pilot had apparently spotted the same waves and opted to return aloft. The giant engines surged to full power as the nose of the aircraft lifted heavenward and climbed back to temporary safety.

Strange, the thoughts that pass through a dying man's mind! I wondered where Mt. Kilimanjaro was. It was probably directly in our path! Oh, why hadn't I spent more time studying my geography? But then, does it really matter where your remains are strewn?

The pilot still had not communicated to us what was going on. Perhaps he didn't know either! But I did know he was circling for another attempt to land. Again he inched his way down through the dense fog. No sight of land or waves yet. I decided he wasn't even looking for a runway . . . he was just trying to locate dirt!

I glanced about me. Almost everyone was still asleep, totally unaware of the great crisis we were encountering. Oh, those poor souls! My sister Myrtle was faithfully manning her window just behind me by now. At least I had a co-pilot! Brother Earl was sound asleep. Ah, the man must live a charmed life. Or maybe God has revealed something to him that has given him this divine tranquility! That's the way it has always been . . . he gets the revelation and I get the sweat!

I looked next to me and there slept Clariece peacefully. God had been merciful to her. He knew she would be terrified if she were awake. So, He let her pass out! I always suspected God really loved her more than me anyway. Now I have proof! I looked down at her hands . . . they were folded. Folded hands! What an omen! I turned back to the window.

Apparently, they had even less equipment to land planes here than back at Dakar. Here they stand a guy on a barrel with a red flag in one hand and a green flag in the other. When he spots you, and hopefully you spot him, he then decides whether you can make it or not. If so, you get a green flag. If not, you get the red one! Very few people ever see the red flag and live to tell about it!

We went through this same routine several times, inching our way down until we spotted the waves. Then we would roar back into the wild blue yonder. Finally, the pilot felt it was time to inform us about what was taking place.

I think I can read voices pretty well. He was

somewhere between major fright and abject terror. He
was trying to sound calm, but I could definitely hear
him whispering the rosary under his breath! He demonstrated an amazing grasp of the obvious . . . it was
too foggy to attempt a landing! Therefore, we would
circle downtown Monrovia until the sun was hot
enough to burn off the fog. Burn, baby, burn!

Here we sat suspended in a holding pattern. I
finally discovered why they refer to it as a "holding"
pattern . . . you hold your breath . . . you hold the
arms of your seat . . . you can't go to the bathroom,
so you also hold everything else! Life stands still!

At this moment you reflect on your life, and
especially your relationship with The Almighty! You
begin to articulate various possibilities of things you
would try to accomplish if God somehow saw fit to
get you out of this. Before long, you are making out-
right vows . . . promises . . . oaths of intentions!

There was no chatter among the passengers. The
only sound was the whine of the jet engines. A few
people were awake, but it didn't seem they fully com-
prehended the gravity of the moment. I listened to
hear sounds. I thought I could hear the pilot whis-
tling *The High and The Mighty* softly from the cockpit. If only we had John Wayne here . . . he would
think of something!

After what seemed an eternity, the fog began to

break up a little. The pilot decided to venture back down to see if he could locate the landing strip. As the plane descended, it was almost as if it were coming down stairs . . . drop, level off, another drop, level off. I could tell he was still "groping" his way down!

Suddenly we broke through the clouds and I could see the earth. No, it was still waves, but land was just ahead. Apparently we were still too low to the water, the pilot lifted back up momentarily before dropping again. This time, I could tell he had committed the craft to an attempted landing.

I felt the tires as they hit the pavement and squealed their announcement that we had indeed touched down. The pilot put on brakes so hard that it almost threw us out of our seats. This runway was apparently designed for much smaller craft!

We taxied to the airport, a small concrete building surrounded by a few shacks. Several old trucks were scattered about, some which seemed to have been abandoned right where their engines had coughed their last breath.

Over to one side, I caught my first glimpse of Nigeria Airways. What I assumed to be its crew was lounging on steps that had been pushed up to the open door of the craft. Shades of Smilin' Jack! I think some of them were actually wearing goggles and leather helmets!

After some of our passengers transferred to the Nigeria Airways plane, we taxied back out for our take off to Lagos. As we taxied down the runway, I was amazed to see children playing on and near the runway! Soon we were aloft for the next 1,000 miles of our trek which would ultimately bring us to Benin City, Nigeria. Benin City . . . the city of blood. Hopefully it wouldn't be mine!

But first, we had to land in Lagos and change to Nigeria Airways. The landing there was also very abrupt, even though this was a fairly large international airport. I never could figure out why all the landings in Africa were so rough. When the door of the plane opened and we stepped outside, the hot humid air almost stiffled me. We left New York on a windy, chilly March day. Here the temperature was about 100 degrees! The "albatross" of heavy wear grew heavier. Do you realize how stupid someone feels carrying a heavy Navy pea jacket in a tropical climate?

Before we disembarked, we were issued some ominous warnings about not taking any photographs. This airport was considered to be a military installation. Anyone taking pictures could be considered a spy. Hey, if I want pictures of the place, I'll buy a postcard! I had already heard some unwary travelers had been incarcerated here for hours for simply taking a few shots with their cameras. So, I was thoroughly convinced to keep my camera totally out of sight!

After clearing customs, we were ushered out to waiting taxicabs. We divided our party into several groups to be transported from the international airport to the domestic airport. I didn't ask questions, I just followed orders. I was assigned a sub-compact vehicle into which squeezed: two couples—McAlister, Bishop Robert and Gloria; Paulk, Donald L. and E. Clariece; one twin sister, Swilley, Darlene; and one semi-civilized cab driver along with enough luggage to supply Hannibal's trek over the Alps!

After we had literally crammed ourselves into this miniature car, someone apparently dropped the green flag! We bolted out of the parking lot like the proverbial bat out of Hades! Please understand that I have taken some wild rides during the course of my life. I have been a passenger in cars driven by legally blind people, cars driven by a wife and a daughter learning to drive, and by an assortment of crazed teenagers in my youth. I have known fear. Plus, I had just flown in a plane whose ability to land was a serious concern. However, this was a significant event! I was being given the single most terrifying ride in my entire life!

This driver was apparently an ex-kamikaze trainee who had been rejected because he was too reckless! It seemed he regarded every other car on the road as his personal enemy trying to keep him from his destination. His mission: seek and destroy. I have heard of defensive driving, but this guy was an expert at aggressive driving!

His car only had one speed . . . wide open! I must say that he was an innovative driver. He realized it was a perfect waste of time to stay in a line of slow moving or stopped traffic. Hence, he pulled out in the passing lane and proceeded at his normal speed (wide open!) toward his destination. As he passed the slower moving cars, I could see the glint in their eyes of sheer hatred that communicated a very real message to me. Given the chance, they would reduce all the inhabitants of our vehicle to become mere statistics of American travelers deceased while traveling abroad! I began to fear that the notorious title of "city of blood" was about to be transferred from Benin City to Lagos!

In the last few hours, my life had flashed before my eyes so many times that I felt as if I had just returned from a family reunion! Again I reflected on any misdeeds I may have committed that I had previously failed to address. I knew this was finally it . . . Doomsday!

I could even imagine what the news report would say back home. A two paragraph blurb would appear on page 23 of the business section that would say: "Local Ass. (a common abbreviation for "assistant") pastor killed in grinding (a word that has always held great terror for me!) car crash in Nigeria. The remains of the late Rev. Ronald J. Paul will be interred tomorrow at a brief ceremony attended by both his friends." And they even misspelled my name!

My mind returns from the obituary page when our driver decides it is time to develop his own roadway. To avoid the oncoming car, he merely leaves the road and continues on the dirt, through yards, around people, until he passes the oncoming car. Then he forces his way back into the line of traffic amid many shouts and much hornblowing and hand signals that I understand very well. They are universal in meaning! There must be a million cab drivers in Lagos and I drew the crowned prince!

Finally, we arrived at the domestic airport. "Domestic," I assume because all flights to and from this airport are within Nigeria. Whatever they may call it, I call it hell! There were soldiers everywhere with their ever-present machine guns. They all looked as if they were in their early teens. From the expression on their faces, they were saying, "Go ahead, make my day!" Just my luck—taken out by an antsy kid suffering with a terminal case of zits!

We were ushered into a building with a low ceiling that seemed to have about 10,000 people milling about. The heat was stifling. The smell of the atmosphere reminded me of odors I preferred to forget! They led us to a side room to retrieve our luggage. This room resembled the chute of a rodeo where wild bulls are unleashed! Behind the wire fence were bags, all just thrown into a giant heap. Some had come open and clothes were strewn about. I tried to see whether I recognized any. Our task was to identify our own luggage, if that were possible!

At this point, I wanted to remind Clariece that I had warned her not to pack so many things, but one glance at her told me she was sick, so I didn't want to say disparaging things to a woman who might be seriously ill! She sat down and muttered, "Water, water." I asked a passerby where I could get some water. I could tell by his expression that I might just as well have asked where Mt. Rushmore was!

I moved her under a ceiling fan for some relief. She had the same pale look on her face that she had worn during her labor before the birth of our first child! Surely she wasn't pregnant! I looked around and saw a scene resembling a war zone.

My twin sister, Darlene, was stretched out on a couch, obviously overtaken with some malady. My other sister, Myrtle, was trying to lend comfort to her while my brother Earl was trying to console Clariece. The McAlisters and Bishop John Meares, veteran travelers, were merely amused by the whole scene.

To further complicate the situation, Brother Earl suddenly suffered a kidney colic attack, a recurring problem with him. That which we feared most had come upon us! He turned the palid color of a mushroom. Sweat began to cascade off his brow.

And what was I doing all this time? I was improving my relationship with the Creator, making some suggestions that we all be supernaturally transported back home! Having been denied this, we all recovered enough to claim our baggage and enter a footrace to our waiting plane. No, it wasn't waiting . . . the crowd waits until they see the plane taxi toward them and they all break loose and run toward it. You see, it is first come, first served!

After we boarded Nigeria Airways and were airborne, the pilot came on the intercom with some interesting comments. He informed us the flying time from Lagos to Benin City was approximately 30 minutes, and we would "try" to land there. I carefully noted the word "try" and wondered exactly what he meant! I was soon to find out. A dense haze settled over the whole area. Sometimes the fog is too dense to see through. Our pilot said he would see how it

looked when we got to Benin City! If it was too dense
to land, we would return to Lagos and travel by car.
Just what I was dying to hear! Maybe we could find
my favorite cabbie to drive us over!

I have my own theory about flying. I think these
pilots learn to fly on the installment plan. They send
away for a book for $9.95 C.O.D. Lesson one teaches
you how to take off. It consists of a series of aerial
photographs showing the earth growing progressively
smaller. Lesson two teaches you how to navigate. It
consists of a series of photographs of objects you do
not wish to strike while airborne. These are photographs of buildings, mountains, and other aircraft.
Lesson three teaches you how to land the plane. It
consists of a series of aerial photographs of the earth
growing progressively larger . . . the photographs
from lesson one simply reversed! I was convinced our
pilot had never gotten to lesson three! He didn't
know how to land this thing! I just knew it!

The plane began to bank to the right. I looked
down to see if I could spot anything through the
haze. Finally I did see something. High tension lines
. . . and they were much too close to us! I felt the
surge of the engines as our pilot obviously spotted
them also, and back up we went. Pass number one.
He circled for another attempt. Now I could see the
ground . . . as a matter of fact, I could see the run-

way. And I could also see that we were still several hundred feet above the runway and we were quickly running OUT of runway! Surely he wouldn't try it this time! There wasn't enough runway left! He didn't try . . . thank God! Once more we surge upward. Pass number two. On the third approach all seemed to be well, but for some reason which I have never understood, he aborted his landing attempt again. On pass number four he finally hit the ground amid squealing tires and applause. Yes, applause! The crew was applauding! I understand this is customary in those countries. But I still suspect that he had just completed his first solo landing! Why else would they carry him off on their shoulders?

We had finally arrived at our destination . . . Benin City, Nigeria. I want to pay special tribute to those who made that trip possible and in many ways contributed to my return to the U.S.A.: First, the other motorists who didn't form a vigilante group and decimate our cab driver and the inhabitants of his car; the soldiers who didn't allow me to "make their day"; the flight attendant who gave me mango juice for sustenance; the electricians who didn't put their power lines any higher; the customs people who didn't think it necessary to strip search me; and especially, I want to thank The Almighty who took mercy on me and brought me back to my children.

I admit I am not a veteran traveler. My idea of a long trip is to travel to Alpharetta, Georgia, or drive fifty miles, whichever comes first. Perhaps in retrospect I must admit that I over-reacted to situations which a seasoned traveler would easily overcome. But if my trip accomplished nothing else, it surely did help me renew my prayer life. Terror caused me to review my past enough so that I hopefully won't make the same mistakes again.

As far as my world travels are concerned, I think I will settle for an occasional jaunt to Stone Mountain. If I'm real adventuresome, I may journey all the way to Lookout Mountain up in Chattanooga. The only way I'll venture abroad again is if God visits me in a burning bush!

Having said that, He will probably send me to Uganda. Come to think about it, that cabbie did resemble Idi Amin . . .

2

SO YOU WANT TO BE A PREACHER?
– February 1986 –

So you want to be a preacher? Sounds like an easy job, huh? After all, as the asinine joke goes, "I woke up this morning craving fried chicken and not wanting to work, so I must be called to preach." Very funny!

O.K. . . . let's change jobs for awhile. All you have to do is face a family whose son has just died of AIDS. Over his sealed coffin you try to speak compassionate words that hopefully will bring them some comfort. Probably the only comfort the family has at this point is the fact their son is finally out of his misery. What would you say . . . God looked down and saw this lovely rose He wanted for His own private garden? Doesn't seem very appropriate, huh? All right! Let's try the old standby. "It is appointed unto man once to die and then the judgment . . ." Just what the bereaved loved ones want to hear . . . more condemnation heaped upon the poor guy!

And then there are the calls from a couple with a young family. A husband and wife with two small children, both under two years of age. They have decided they can't make it work any longer. They are calling the marriage quits. And what about the kids? Who is going to be around to explain to them what is happening with Mommy and Daddy?

And how about the young husband who has just discovered his wife has developed a relationship with another man? It seems she finds her new-found relationship to be more fulfilling. But then, maybe the young husband had unknowingly asked for this to happen by his inconsiderate and insensitive actions. He never offered her anything of himself except inconsistencies and immaturity. She only wanted a man she could depend on, one who would remain the same day after day. She now thinks she has found it in an older man. Well, at least they don't have any children to leave devastated! Have any words of wisdom for any of the parties involved?

Now let's go to the funeral of a fellow minister and his wife, both tragically killed in an automobile accident. Both caskets rest side by side before his own pulpit. Yes, he kept the faith . . . Yes, he finished his course. But tell that to his four children. Somehow the profundity of the providential hand of God doesn't matter to the kid who only knows he doesn't have a dad to play ball with him anymore . . . or a mother to kiss away the hurts. One fell swoop, and they are both gone! Still want to be a preacher?

Oh, and lest we forget, you have the great joy of counseling with people who have run out of money as well as places or people to find any. You are their last resort. The rent is several months past due. The gas and water have already been disconnected. There is nothing in the house to eat . . . and they have five hungry, tattered kids waiting in an old clunker outside, noses pressed against the cold window glass with fear written all over their little dirty faces! Being a minister is so much fun!

Others have simply lost the will to live. They would take their own lives, but they can't figure out how to do it painlessly. They simply settle for a living death.

I remember another very thrilling event you may want to recall the next time you wonder what your preacher really does for a living. A young unwed mother is having second thoughts about giving up her newborn child for adoption to a Christian couple. Understandable. She has natural motherly instincts. She is a young teenager, however, who will have great difficulty pulling her life back together with an infant to raise.

She admits she is looking forward to getting back with her teenage friends and finding a boyfriend. But how do you date with a small baby in your arms? Her uncertain heart whispers, "The baby is yours! Keep it."

Meanwhile, a childless couple has tirelessly prayed for years to receive a baby. They have been interviewed, screened thoroughly with a fine-toothed comb, and have proved they can provide an excellent Christian home for the baby. The nursery has been made ready . . . now they just wait for the blessed event to occur. Would you like to break the news to them that the young mother has changed her mind?

After a tearful session with the teenager, she finally listens to reason rather than her heart and decides to surrender the child. And guess who has to take that baby from her arms, all the while knowing she will never see her baby again? Right . . . your basic 9 to 5 pastor! No, make that your 12 to 12 pastor!

And speaking of teenage unwed mothers, what about the thirteen-year-old who became pregnant by her mother's boyfriend while the mother was at work? And . . . are you ready for this? . . . the mother wants to keep the child and raise it as the girl's sister! I just know you have an instant solution for this one!

By now, you may be asking what you get for all of this fun? Well, you get to live in a glass house. After all, everyone knows that a preacher isn't an ordinary human . . . he is a very special breed. So, he is put in a place where his every move can be observed and critiqued. Judgment is passed on all his friends . . . just to help him decide who he should and should not associate with.

Then there is the question of salary. This is the touchy part. Many people feel he should receive no salary at all, then there are others who want to keep it as low as possible . . . "to keep him humble!" Strangely, most of the people who question the preacher's salary don't even pay tithes! They occasionally tip God a buck or so and feel that gives them the privilege to direct the finances of the church. Boy, we're havin' a good time now!

You are trying to find compensations. Right? The preacher does get to set his own schedule, doesn't he? Sure, all he has to do is stay on call twenty-four hours a day. And, oh how I always love those middle-of-the-night calls. These callers fall in several different categories.

First, those who are drunk. A drunk usually has three basic responses that time of the night. He either wants to (a) fight, (b) make love, or (c) get religious! And I have yet to see one who could do any of those three things properly while inebriated! After he sobers up, a preacher is the last person he wants to talk with, but in the middle of the night, he is the one person who will talk after everyone else has lost patience.

Then there are those souls who are alone and frightened. They hear all those scary things that go bump in the night and they just need to hear a gentle voice reassuring them that they will make it 'til daybreak . . . and may they please call again if they hear more noises? They wait apprehensively for dawn, which by the way, solves many ghastly problems. With the rising of the morning sun, they discover things were really not as bleak as they had seemed.

I could go on for pages extolling the many exciting reasons to consider the ministry. Like being able to sit on the stage where everyone can watch you fight sleep because you are dead tired from spending the night at the emergency room with a wreck victim, or better still, someone with the D.T.'s . . . helping him get rid of the big green spiders crawling on him. Lest I sound like I'm complaining, let me quickly list some fringe benefits. You get a reserved parking spot! Now that alone should make you want to enroll in seminary today!

By now, you may be asking the question "Is it

really worth it?" Once I was in a meeting with an internationally known minister. He broke down and cried like a baby and told about 400 of us fellow ministers that he just didn't want to be a preacher anymore. We all knew why he was crying . . . and we were crying with him!

All I can say is that if you want to be a preacher, you'd better know that you know that you know God has called you! Otherwise, you won't last very long! And even if you are sure beyond a shadow of a doubt, times still come when you feel like telling them to "take this job and shove it!" There are those days I would gladly change places with the 9 to 5 guy who sells shoes, then goes home and forgets about things 'til tomorrow. At least, there would be no midnight emergency calls, no visits to jails to see the frightened captives peering through the bars wondering what is going to happen to them, no death messages to deliver to unsuspecting families . . .

Why do we keep on? Well, there is this scripture that says something about the callings of God being without repentance. The rough translation of that is "Woe is me if I don't preach!"

So, tomorrow morning I will arise and once again put on my collar. Ah, the collar . . . it shouts to the world who you are. Then it provides the golden opportunity to pray in bus stations with people who just come up to you crying and begging, "Father, please pray for me!" And with a collar, you dare not refuse to let everyone go first in traffic. But still, I will don the collar and resume the Father's business!

Next Sunday I will sit and search the faces of the congregation. And again I will ask myself the question, "Is it really worth it?" And again, my answer will unhesitatingly be "Yes!" . . . Why?

Because I see the face of one who came to me as a young man involved in a homosexual lifestyle. His life is changed. Today he is married and the father of a beautiful child. Because I see a couple who were about to throw in the towel but decided to stick it out a little longer. So far, so good. At least the kids have live-in parents!

I see face after face of those whose lives have been salvaged from the trash heap of life. And because I see myself. I was at the top of that pile! No, I was not a murderer or drunkard, but I desperately, though unknowingly, tried to self-destruct in more ways than one! Somehow, God just wouldn't turn me loose. I still don't have all the answers or solutions, but at least I see the light at the end of the tunnel.

Every preacher has his own calling and develops his own style of ministering; or at least he should. I would be a fool to attempt to duplicate another's style and methods. Some can minister from behind the pulpit to thousands. Me . . . I'm more comfortable one on one. And I am most comfortable behind a typewriter. That is a pulpit to me.

Well, the next time you hear someone knocking the local parson, just remember, it ain't as easy as it looks! Now please don't get me wrong. I'm not complaining . . . I just needed a soft shoulder to cry on and besides . . . I had a few minutes to kill before the funeral starts . . .

3

THE SOCK DEMON
– September 1986 –

For years I have suspected my house, like many others, was occupied by some dark force which prowled the back rooms wreaking havoc. It's not that my house is literally haunted, it's just that certain things always seem to go wrong.

Now no less a spiritual giant than Jamie Buckingham has admitted that his house, too, is occupied by some dark denizen. Jamie's admission that he has a "sock-gobbling" demon at large in his house has given many of us the necessary courage to come forth and openly admit our problems. It's the only way we will ever find solutions! Individually, we cower . . . united, we strike back!

Socks. Although people usually assume that every well dressed man wears them, more and more I am seeing the hairy ankles of young men who have revolted against this tradition. I often wondered what great thrill they received from this practice, so I tried it on a couple of casual occasions such as running to the store or the service station. After all, I couldn't show up in the pulpit sockless without some serious experimentation to see if this new style would enhance my sartorial image! But when I tried it, I felt as naked as if I had left home without my trousers! I just knew every eye I met was focused on my nude ankles!

And so I must continue to deal with the issue of socks in my life. The devil knows this is not an option but a necessity. That is where he always strikes . . . where he knows there are no options. Therefore, I have become one of those poor souls whose life has fallen prey to a habit.

Like most other sensible men, I select my daily attire starting with my socks. If I can find two reasonably compatible black socks, then I go with a black or gray suit. If I find blue socks, I can move into a blue serge or perhaps even my navy blazer. If I can't locate either, I have been known to resort to white socks and white shoes. This, I might add, is a last resort and applies only before Labor Day. I have been warned that you don't "do" white after that date. And when I am forced to "do" white, I get strange sideways glances from those in my household who are astute in fashion etiquette . . . which seems to be everyone but me! They don't come right out and question my sanity, but they certainly do question several other things, including my eyesight, my taste, my awareness of the twentieth century and my willingness to embarrass them!

But back to the underlying cause of this whole mess . . . the sock demon. I am convinced this thing has inhabited my premises for years. In fact, I really believe it resided at our last address. When we moved, it simply came along as a stowaway.

Because I did not want to appear to be a religious fanatic, at first I would casually ask where my missing sock was. I wouldn't come right out and say there was a demonic spirit at work here. I simply hoped my questions would alert the other spiritual people in my household. Supposedly, they would catch the drift of my suspicions and activate their discernment to help me identify the culprit. After all, if any two of us are agreed as touching . . . Oh well, you know all about that!

It didn't work! I was made aware of all the natural phenomena that usually explains these occurrences. Oh, the mind of reason! It is so hard for the carnal mind to comprehend spiritual things! "Haven't you ever heard of static cling?" I was asked. "Did you check Donnie Earl's drawer?" "You probably left them in your shoes . . . did you look under the couch?" They just don't understand the gravity of "spiritual warfare!"

I do know about static cling . . . and the products available to control it. I do know I have carelessly removed my socks and left them at various locations in the house. I do know I have a teenage son who is a prime suspect with his size twelve feet. But all this still doesn't account for the loss of all my socks. I have tried everything. I threw all my socks away and started over with a new batch. It didn't work. Before a month had passed, I went to my drawer and pulled it open only to see dozens of socks that were total strangers to one another! I talked it over with them. They didn't seem to know how it had happened! Don't you see what has happened? I stand before an open drawer carrying on a conversation with socks . . . and expecting a reply! I AM in trouble!

Lest you think I have blown the whole issue out of proportion, let me try to explain why this is important to me and my ministry. Consider my schedule. I am a relatively busy man. I have a fairly tight schedule, especially on certain days. Take Sunday, for instance.

In order to arrive at church on time to assume

my position as a spiritual leader, I must adhere to a strict itinerary. Six people reside at my house using 2½ bathrooms in a period of approximately 93 minutes! My allotted share of this time is approximately 15½ minutes. I know exactly how long it takes me to shower. I have perfected shaving to a science . . . exactly 34 strokes (unless I have a phone call and lose my place), I know how long it takes to dry my hair . . . which, by the way, is taking less time every morning!

So, to stay on my schedule, I can't afford any unexpected snafu such as "sock loss." I open my sock drawer and begin my daily search. Here is where my first prayer of the day usually occurs . . . "God, let there be black!" Instead I find 57 assorted socks of various brands, hues, fabrics and sizes. Now, if you have any basic working knowledge of higher mathematics, you immediately realize something is amiss when you come up with an odd number of anything coming in pairs! Obviously I, too, have a "sock-gobbling" demon!

I try to narrow the search to similar colors and materials. Brand matches aren't even necessary at this point . . . just two black socks, that's all I ask! And if I am extremely fortunate, I can locate two that are free of holes!

After locating several candidates, I must make

the final judgment. To do this, I must have a good light, preferably natural sunlight. Flourescent lighting is tremendously deceptive, leading to untold misery! Soft closet light also presents definite problems. You are probably wondering why I don't turn on the overhead light.

That is a good question and deserves an answer. Simple. I hate overhead lights! I suspect that is one of the places demons hide when they aren't doing their dastardly deeds in the washing machine! And in addition to that, I have discovered that my marriage runs much more smoothly when I keep a low profile in the early morning hours, especially if Clariece is still sleeping! An overhead light suddenly turned on in the eyes of a sleeping woman doesn't ensure domestic tranquility!

So, I drape several socks over my arm. Looking like a transient clothes line, I search for an uncovered window that will allow some natural light in for my divination. If the day is overcast, you may encounter difficulty in making a proper analysis. Pray for bright sunlight . . . that is always the best!

If you are in doubt, there are a few little things that may help. Gold toes are a blessing. At least they identify brand similarities. Check for elastic strength to narrow down the approximate decade of the manufacture.

I might add yet another pitfall. On certain days we are forced to arise before the sun. I honestly try to be objective here, folks. I believe that God has everything pretty well figured out. He knew that man needed light to perform important functions in life. For light, He provided the sun. God Himself selected the hour at which the sun begins to provide that light each day. Why should I grow impatient and get ahead of God? Man should never get up before God Himself has ordained that day begins.

I have enough trouble making it when the sun arrives! I try so hard to see the beauty of sunrises, and even though I admit they are lovely, to me they are no lovelier than sunsets, which come at a much more decent hour! After all, they're the same thing, just on the other end of the sky! How much beauty can one person hope to enjoy on any given day? I appreciate sunsets and am content. When you are out enjoying the sunrises, feel free to enjoy it vicariously for me!

Back to the issue at hand . . . make that at foot! After selecting what hopefully is a match, and completing quickly the rest of my dressing, I am ready to go. Clariece contends that when her hair is done, she is 95% dressed. With me, it is socks! When I am able to locate clean, matching socks, I'm practically garbed!

The real test of sock selection comes at a critical time . . . on the platform when thousands of people stare at your feet in the glare of TV lights. You know they are staring. You can feel their eyes!

I casually allow my eyes to drift downward. Not too fast, or I may attract the attention of those few people who haven't noticed yet! I can identify with the prophet who said, "That which I feared most has come upon me." I see to my deep chagrin a black sock and an imposter . . . a deep blue sock!

Multiplied thousands of eyes have made the same discovery. The television crew has found out about it. I can hear them on the headsets . . . "Get a close-up of Pastor Don's socks. He has done it again!" Little children in the front row are giggling. Someone whispers the news to a blind member . . . and she is laughing!

Now everyone's imagination goes crazy! They assume one of three things: (a) they suspected all along that Pastor Don was color blind. Affirmed! (b) they suspected all along that Pastor Don was a fashion slob. Affirmed! (c) they suspected all along that Pastor Don's marriage was in trouble. If Clariece really loved him, she wouldn't let him out of the house looking like that! The marriage is GONE. Affirmed! Pass the word!

You see, these poor misguided souls never stop

to consider that there is clearly a demon at work here. They are witnessing the sad demise of a family who fails to discern the demon in time. Now it is too late. Perhaps, if when they were first married . . . But here sits the shell of a man, reduced to a quivering hulk by the subtle destructive deeds of the "sock gobbling" demon! It isn't a pretty sight!

Now, I fear this demon will spread to other areas of my domicile. Already I am beginning to spot little suspicious traces of his work elsewhere. I leave my collar buttons neatly placed on my dresser within the protective circle of my sacred collar. Maybe if I placed my cross with them . . . During the night they have either sprouted tiny little legs, or the demon has transported them elsewhere. I know where I left my buttons!

Other items are vanishing mysteriously also . . . nail clippers, tooth brushes, scissors, flashlights. Some reappear just as mysteriously, while others are gone forever . . . perhaps through the "black hole!"

I try to approach this whole issue scientifically and find the reasonable answer. I have developed my own procedure to ascertain whether it is a genuine metaphysical occurrence, or indeed, even some logical explanation. First, I retrace my steps to see whether I have overlooked that one ingredient that will provide the answer. Occasionally, I do find a logical explanation. But, often there just isn't one!

In order to appreciate my plight, you have to believe that I am not your basic careless person. As a child I was schooled to be very careful and protective of items entrusted to me. That training has carried over. Whenever you see me, you can pretty much depend upon me having two things in my possession at that moment. One is my keys, and the other is my wallet. I used to have a third item, a little Swiss Army knife, but the demon absconded with that long ago!

The younger generation just doesn't understand this type of responsibility. Perhaps it is because new designer jeans don't provide proper pocket space. I realize jeans are also probably too tight to allow a hand to insert or extract any item larger than a "fro pick," which more or less "hangs" from a rear pocket.

I have observed the younger generation with much interest. My beloved nephew and the youth pastor of our church has kept the entire staff/non-staff stocked with keys and wallets for years by leaving them unintentionally at various places. You could usually track him down by the trail of items he couldn't or wouldn't put in his pockets!

I have provided no less than a dozen house keys to my teenage son, Donnie Earl. Do you know how he gets into the house? He goes to a pay phone and calls me collect! And whatever happened to the quarter I gave him this morning to make any necessary phone call? I watched him drop it down into his sock just this morning . . . oh, now I am beginning to get the picture! The sock demon again . . .

And speaking of keys, there is also a demon of "key proliferation." Did you know that? If you are anywhere near our church and need access, all you have to do is stop the first stranger you meet on the sidewalk and he can probably produce a master key to the entire plant!

As you can well see, we have a problem here. I contend it is a spiritual problem! Jamie, you have unearthed a monster. Where will it all end? If we allow this to go unchecked, just think . . . today socks and keys . . . tomorrow our copy of *The Seduction of Christianity*, a book that attempts to identify the evil spirits that lurk all about us. Now if the authors, Messrs. Hunt and McMahan are seriously interested in finding subtle demons that plague the Church, let them start here! After all, these are attacking the very elect!

And with any success, they may discover a new cult within the Church. This one worships single socks . . . The Single Sock Sect! As for me, if I have one more sock "seduced" away, I will be tempted to start my own church—one teaching socks are of the devil! Selah!

4

AMANDA
–August 1986–

Amanda Bogart

There are some spiritual giants who seem to have many answers to the questions of life. I am not one of them. I am a sojourner. I travel the same path as other pilgrims, encounter the same pains and anxieties, and ask the same questions. Some say we have no right to ask "why?" about things that seem to be within the providence of God. My guess is, when doors close at night and wise men lie upon their beds to reflect, they too ask the same questions.

Little Amanda died. Why? Because she had cancer, that's why. It seems so cold to say it that way. After all, she was only ten years old. Why couldn't it have been one of us who has lived most of our lives? Give the kid a break . . . let her live!

Could we have done more? What else can we do after we have committed her to a loving, unerring

God? Spiritually, we did all we knew to do. We prayed, fasted, cried, claimed, rebuked, promised, adjured, loosed, bound . . . everything . . . but still she died. Why?

She received the finest medical care available. She underwent all the treatments, the surgeries . . . everything science could provide was administered . . . yet Amanda died. Why?

She fought a good fight and kept the faith. She never complained or asked questions as to why she had been stricken. It seems God often gives the young a tranquility that surpasses their tender years. Perhaps it's because they don't have much to compare life with at that point. They just assume disease and pain is something we all face . . . a part of life . . . par for the course.

I really don't care to hear that diatribe about God walking in His garden, spotting this beautiful little rose, and deciding to pick it for His own. It's not that beautiful at all. Amanda had cancer and died. It's that simple. Cancer! A dreaded curse of Satan that strikes the young, the old, the rich, the poor . . . knowing no boundaries. It reaches into most of our homes sooner or later. There is nothing pretty about it.

And yet, there was beauty that surrounded Amanda's death. Beauty in the serenity of a mother, father and sister who understood that if their only hope was this life, they would be miserable people. Beauty in the love of a family standing constantly by Amanda's bed with cheerful smiles on their faces, their hope transmitting to Amanda that a miracle could be right around the corner. But also beauty in the tears of love they shed when their backs were turned from her.

I watched the Body of Christ at work . . . pastors standing by, doing everything possible to ease the pain . . . friends who came just to assure the family that they were praying. I saw Sharalee Lucas sing over Amanda's little semi-conscious body, and watched a minor miracle occur. Somehow, that little soul reached out through unconsciousness. For a fleeting moment, spirit touched spirit. Deep called unto deep.

Amanda was an extraordinarily beautiful child. She had dancing eyes and a smile for everyone she met . . . even throughout her terminal sickness. It is easy after someone is gone to extol his virtues and recall his many good points. However, in Amanda's case, even before her death anyone could see that she was a special little girl. Everyone's child is special, but when cancer robs us of young ones, the tragedy seems more acute.

My baby sister was a victim of cancer. She also died. I had questions then. If there ever was a pure soul, it was Joan, my little sister. And yet she died. Why? I don't know. But then maybe that's the way God intended it to be for the time being. After all, isn't there a scripture that tells us that we see through a glass darkly? Perhaps God knows our finite minds just couldn't comprehend the answers anyway.

After my sister died, something happened that made me accept, if not understand, some of my questions. My parents are older now. They have difficulty remembering things. One morning about 3 a.m. I found my dad out in the yard with a flashlight. I asked him what he was doing. He told me he was looking for Joan. He explained that she had been gone for several hours, and he and Mama were worried about her. He was trying to find her.

I led him back into the house where Mama sat on the couch. I always try to be as gentle as possible when telling them a family member is dead. Each time they hear the news, it is as if they are hearing it for the first time . . . a death message. I gently said to Mama, "Joan died about a year ago. I guess we forgot about it for a moment."

And then, for a moment I saw a "knowing" look come over her face. I hadn't seen that look in years. It was as though she'd suddenly returned to days when her memory was intact. Then she made a very profound statement. "Maybe that's the way God intended for it to be . . . for us to forget so that we won't worry."

Maybe so. It's as good an answer as I have heard lately! God in His mercy cushions the blows of life in subtle ways. As we grow older, our family and friends begin to die. After awhile, we just can't seem to remember the pain.

Jesus was asked the same questions we ask today. "Who sinned?" they asked Him when He encountered an afflicted lad. Does God punish us for our wickedness by inflicting sickness and death upon our innocent children? If I believed that, I would never darken the door of another church! I am a man with all the natural emotions others experience. That includes revenge. But I wouldn't punish an innocent child to repay an adult. Don't try to tell me God does that either!

What is death? It is a curse that was cast upon man when he disobeyed God. In that sense, we are all guilty . . . the entire human race, including women and children. But there has to be an answer . . . a solution.

And there is an answer. Surprisingly, the answer is easy, even obvious! The answer to all of man's suffering and death is the restoration of the Kingdom of God on earth, even as it is in heaven. It is the return to the estate man enjoyed in the Garden of Eden.

Wishful thinking, you say? No, not really. Not if you really believe God is everything we preach and teach and sing He is. Sometimes I don't think we believe the stories we tell our children about an omnipotent God! Either that, or we just don't believe what we read in the Bible! But that is another story for another time.

The last enemy to be destroyed is death. We are engaged in a battle to the death with death, if you please! If we don't give up, we will win. Amanda did her part. She struck a mighty blow at death as she went. He didn't frighten her, or take away her joy or her peace. She looked him squarely in the eye and said, "Give me your best shot, Satan. You don't scare me!"

Little by little some of us are beginning to understand that we are in a battle that CAN be won! I don't have all the answers, but I know this is true. The generation could well be just around the corner who will face death, look in his ugly, grotesque face, and refuse to give in. The prize . . . eternal life! After all, God promised it would be that way!

Often we can almost hear the spirits of loved ones speaking back to us from beyond. If Amanda could speak, I think I hear what she would say to us . . .

"*Don't weep for me, family and friends,*
Even though I know how you loved me,
I knew your love and it was my source of
Strength.
I saw your smile to encourage me, but I
Knew you cried when you turned away . . .
Weep no more, for all is well now and
My body is perfect.
The stories you told me that you hoped
Were true, they are indeed true.
Weep for yourselves if you must weep,
For your battle rages on.
Fight a good fight and keep the faith.
Rest assured that victory is just in sight.
What is heaven like? Oh, I can't tell you all
Right now, for you would be so discontent
Where you are.
It is peaceful.
It is joy.
It is beautiful beyond your imagination.
The rainbow that swirls around the throne,
The choir that sings, the Light that shines . . .
Please don't weep, though I know you will,
For mortal flesh is pained in the loss of mortal
Flesh.
Just know, it is the Kingdom of God pure and

Simple you seek;
Not a theological treatise,
Not a doctrine to espouse or defend,
Not a tradition to extend.
You seek a place with God Himself where tears
  Will be wiped away and there will be no
  Separation, no sickness, no pain, no death.
Where am I? I am at hand, I am a heartbeat away,
  I am here for the taking . . . for I represent
  The Kingdom to you . . .
That you can understand.
Seek me . . . long for me . . . I am a treasure laid
  Up where there is no corruption, but all is at rest.
I am at rest. All is well. I await you.
So weep not, my loved ones, weep not . . .

5

NO SMOKING
– October 1986 –

There is little need for a "no smoking" sign inside a sanctuary. However, I recall several years ago when a lady attended our church who happened to be a chain-smoker. She was so accustomed to smoking that she had already fired up a cigarette in the church service before her friend reminded her where she was!

Since I don't go many places other than church, "no smoking" sections have never really been a big item with me! I see "non-smoking" areas in restaurants, but usually patrons are so involved in satisfying their appetite for food they can forego the nicotine habit for a while. The point being, I hadn't really thought too much about the "problem" until I was faced with it recently. Let me tell you my story.

I flew on what ordinarily is a relatively short plane trip from Jacksonville to Atlanta. Flying time:

approximately forty-five minutes. Little did I know that it would seem more like forty-five hours!

I might add that forty-five minutes doesn't include the time you sit on the ground awaiting take-off, which in this instance was another thirty-five minutes. I might also add that this is usually the worst part of the trip for me. I will elaborate.

Let me preface this elaboration with the comment that I never really begrudge the time spent on the ground if they are actually using that time to make sure the plane is airworthy! I definitely do not want them to take ANY shortcuts when it comes to maintenance. That could cause an adverse effect on "my missile" while it is airborne 35,000 feet above terra firma! I want them to check and recheck every single inch of that contraption. After all, I have a personal vested interest in this project . . . my life!

As you may know, the smoking sections of most planes are in the very rear, with the exception of first class passengers who pay another extra hundred bucks or so just to sit up front in slightly larger seats, have the privilege of being served first, getting off the plane first . . . AND smoking up front!

I don't have any idea how it happened, but for some reason I was assigned a seat in the "smoking" section of the plane. In addition to that, Clariece had been assigned a seat on the other side of the aisle. Now I have learned after twenty-five years of marriage that I CAN actually be separated from Clariece for stretches up to forty-five minutes without it jeopardizing my life or our relationship! However, I am not the happiest flier in the world! I do like to sit next to a prayer warrior who will join with me in deep intercession for the health and sanity of the pilot. Plus, in this case, it would ensure that there would at least be a non-smoker on one side of me. There are other reasons I like her close by, some of which include last minute confessions if I become aware that the plane is going to crash!

As we moved to the rear of the plane, we realized our seats were two rows from the very back. It was one of those long planes. I really don't want to learn the names of planes because I don't care to know them personally! I am amused, however, by veteran travelers who can rattle off "this is a DC9" or "today we are flying the D27!" I only know we are inside a huge piece of metal that somehow is supposed to leave the ground and fly like a bird! I know feathers can fly, but I contend that metal can't pull off this amazing feat! What actually happens is that you are strapped to a virtual rocket and shot from one place to another like a bullet. If you are getting the impression that I am afraid to fly, you are wrong. It is not the flying that bothers me. It's the crashing and burning I worry about!

O.K. There I was, seated in the back of this long metal tube. Now, please understand that I have a very active imagination when being restrained in a projectile such as this, waiting to be hurled into the sky at speeds that God never intended man to travel. Actually, I don't think God really wants man to travel any faster than he can run! The fatality rate at speeds higher than that ought to confirm that premise!

I looked down the long fuselage of the plane. I estimated that it was approximately 7,000 feet from me to the nearest open exit at the front of the plane! Between me and that only opening were teeming thousands . . . multitudes . . . hordes of people, every one of them using up all available oxygen before it could reach me!

I don't have severe claustrophobia, but suffice it to say I don't like to be confined in extremely close places! I try to avoid this whenever possible. In these situations, I have to conduct stern conversations with myself in order that I don't act like a total fool! I was engaged in such a conversation at this very moment! "People will think you are crazy if you tear your clothes off and run up the aisle screaming for oxygen!" I listened intently to my own logic which indeed made sense!

Other conditions began to complicate the situation. I am sure mechanical geniuses can tell me the reason, but when a plane is sitting waiting to crank its engines, the air that comes out those little nozzles over your head is not cold air! At best, it is cool, and occasionally it is even warm! At this point, I needed all the oxygen possible! I felt as if I were going to hyperventilate and do something crazy. I aimed all three nozzles toward my face. It was useless . . . only a slight zephyr wafted out!

I didn't say anything to Clariece. I always want her to think of me as a strong man who can leap tall buildings in a single bound! But I felt as if I were going to pass out. I bent over as if to check my socks, (I was glad to see they matched!) but actually, I was trying to get some blood to my head or whatever it is that is supposed to happen when you put your head between your knees.

I spoke even more sternly to myself! "Listen dummy, do you know what will happen if you pass out? Some fat lady will scream and everyone will immediately think, 'Fire!' Mass hysteria will break out. Your already unconscious body will be trampled to death by the herd making for the nearest exit . . . 7,000 feet away!"

I began feeling a little better with my head down, so I ventured to come back up to assess the situation. Clariece was oblivious to my distress. I glanced over at her and saw she was reading a book entitled, *The Queen of Peace Visits Medugorje*. Little did she realize that seated across the aisle, "The King of Paranoia" was just about to visit the twilight zone! I thought, "Here I am on the verge of being rendered unconscious and she is only interested in apparitions that appear to ten year old girls." I wondered how she would feel when she saw an apparition of her departed husband appearing on the wing of this "D" whatever it is?

And to make matters worse, I was seated in the midst of a zone reserved for nicotine addicts! As the passengers made their way to their seats, I surveyed each one who walked down the aisle. I like to sit by people who don't want to talk. I prefer enjoying my misery alone! Soon a grandmotherly looking little lady came down the aisle, looking up through her bifocals, reading the seat numbers. She stopped in the aisle when she recognized her seat number next to me. I thought I had been spared! By another mistake they had surely placed a returned missionary by me!

When at last everyone was seated, I assumed we could take off. Wrong assumption! Just because all the seats are full, that does not necessarily mean takeoff is imminent! It only means all the seats are full!

I had several revelations during this ordeal. First, I discovered that for the most part, smokers look like everyone else. But there are some basic differences. For one thing, they don't believe that sitting in the "smoking" section only provides them with an option to smoke. It means they are OBLIGATED to smoke. I also learned that people who request seats in the smoking section are not just casual smokers . . . they are SERIOUS smokers! The expressions on their faces reminded me of condemned prisoners on death row smoking their final cigarettes on earth before their executions!

Everyone nervously refrained from smoking during the takeoff, but I noticed they all held a cigarette and lighter in their hands and kept their eyes glued to the "smoking/no-smoking" indicator. You could almost sense the countdown! It was like sprinters settling in their starting blocks . . . "on your mark, get set . . . smoke!" As soon as the "No Smoking" light was turned off, I heard the lighters click in unison, firing up cigarettes. I felt the intense heat generated and heard the combined suction of air rush into all the polluted lungs about me.

As I looked up and saw clouds of smoke hovering all around me, my eyes began to water. I felt as if I would choke. I watched the smoke exiting the other

passengers mouths and nostrils, making its way
snakelike toward me. I held my breath as long as possible, but I realized I couldn't hold my breath for the
entire flight. I would eventually have to come up for
air. I don't relish the thought of drinking water that
has been in someone else's mouth . . . why would I
want to share their discarded smoke?

"Surely the little grandmother beside me will
not be a smoker," I silently hoped. Then she opened
her purse. I just knew she was going to extract her
little New Testament to enjoy some short devotional
reading. Wrong! She pulled out her leather encased
pack of Virginia Slims! (And from the looks of this
lady, she had come an extremely long way . . .
BABY!) My heart sank! Was there no knee left
unbowed to Baal on the earth?

To add to my disillusionment, when the flight
attendant came around, asking what we wanted to
drink, this little grandmother ordered a fine pilsner
beer, whatever that is! I sat there watching this little
lady, sucking on her cancer stick and drinking her
brew. I wondered how old she was. How could she
have lived this long and smoked that much? By the
way, I also discovered people in the smoking section
don't smoke just one cigarette. They smoke one right
after another as long as the smoking lamp is lit. I
almost decided to risk asking her how old she was,

but I was afraid she would do one of two things, both
of which were bad. One, she might tell me it was
none of my business and pull out a chain saw and
waste me on the spot . . . or, worse still, she would
tell me she was only 25! My, how smoking and drinking . . . and flying will age you . . .

6

OLD SOLDIERS
DO DIE
– May 1984 –

Earl P. Paulk, Sr. and son

Addie Mae and Earl Paulk

Ef every man is expected to master only one craft in life, then this man was a total success. His craft . . . preaching. There had been a divine call upon his life, and he heard that call and applied himself to carry out the sacred mission entrusted him. Others have heard that same divine voice through the centuries and have responded to the call. One who heard that call and responded was Earl Pearly Paulk, Sr. He is my father.

I suppose every vocation has those whose work becomes a benchmark for others to emulate. Earl Paulk was such a standard. Even today, literally hundreds of preachers pattern their ministries after this unique man.

I look at Daddy now, an old soldier of the Cross, and it brings so many emotions to me. General Douglas MacArthur quoted a line when he returned from the battles of world wars that had taken him literally around the world . . . the Philippines, Japan, Korea. I was just a young boy when I heard him say with his voice breaking, "Old soldiers never die . . . they just fade away." And, as the saying goes, even though this old soldier has not died, he has indeed faded.

As I said, he learned only one craft. I don't point this out to his discredit. He was totally consumed by his divine mission. I don't ever recall seeing him drive a nail, hang a picture or do many of the mechanical or manual things usually expected of men. He saw to it that they were done, but he always had far more important things to do than serve as a handyman around the house. As I look back now, I have questions. I ask, "Was it fair to ever expect him to retire? After all, he didn't really know how to do anything except preach!"

It's not that he didn't work hard. He kept a pace that would have killed lesser men. It's just that he was burning with this one task in life . . . to preach the gospel. He was never really interested in anything else. Oh, he used to talk a great deal about other things like hunting and fishing. He never got the opportunity to do very much of either because of his busy schedule. Probably the greatest joy he derived from those pastimes was just being able to talk about them and dream about having a change of activity. As a matter of fact, after he retired to his little farm, to my knowledge he never went hunting one time. He fished only a few times just to placate a pleading grandchild.

God called him to preach when he was still a teenage farm boy. After his "call," the whole community recognized a dramatic change in his life, for he was instantly transformed from a religious cynic to a flaming evangelist.

The "hand" upon his life carried him far beyond his beloved South Georgia fields, eventually taking him to preach around the world. The stories about his ministry will fill a book . . . and I say "will." I hope someday to chronicle a book on his life as "one of the greats."

But for the moment I want to see him as he is, an old soldier who deserves a moment of attention . . . a salute, if you will! He is eighty years old now. Even though he is physically alive, in many ways he is living proof that old soldiers may not die. But they do fade into a sort of oblivion.

He retired when he was sixty-three. There was a time when I thought that "sixty-three" was old! I am in my late forties . . . now sixty-three just doesn't seem that old. As a matter of fact, he had probably reached the age when he could finally exercise the mature judgment only years of experience bring.

Retirement was probably the worst sentence he could have received, but he had no choice. In our society we cater to the notion that youth must be served . . . and served now! It's the old "move over and give me my turn" syndrome. Young cubs lurk impatiently, waiting for the old lions to fall by the wayside so they can become kings of the jungle!

Daddy always said that when he retired he would show his peers how it should be done. You see, he knew "old lions" who even though they had seen their days, still insisted on coming around to sound their threatening roars. This didn't set very well with the young ones!

Daddy never wanted to do this. When he was gone, he would let the replacements have their day in the sun without his interference. And he was as good as his word! When his time came, he went quietly, and proceeded to fade away . . . not only from the world in which he had once lived, but deep within himself. In doing so, he also lost his purpose for living.

For the first few years he kept a light schedule. For a short time, he served as "minister of visitation" in his local hometown church, a position created to give old men something to keep them busy and out of the way. He had been a general official in his denomination. Now a list of people to visit was handed to him by a man whose very career had depended on Daddy's decisions just a few days earlier!

Daddy could see through this ploy. His professional pride would not allow him to continue, though he still desperately needed to touch . . . to minister to people. Finally, he opted to sit it out for the duration. He went to the farm for good.

No longer did he receive calls to preach at campmeetings or to participate in high-level executive sessions deciding church policy. He was relegated to a little farm in South Georgia. Now his greatest responsibility was to gather pecans and feed some stray cats that Mama allowed to gather at her doorstep. The old firehorse had been put out to pasture. When he heard the "fire-bell," his ears would still perk up. But he resisted the urge to gallop to the blaze!

Little by little, we watched the call that had so deeply burned within him begin to wane. There were some physical complications, but it seemed he really didn't have the will to fight any longer. He developed diabetes. He was forced to go on a stringent diet and later, to take insulin daily. Probably the one vice he had allowed to any degree in his life was overindulging in eating. Now, even this was no longer enjoyable

to him. It was almost as if everything he had once
lived for had been taken from him!

I recall those earlier days when attending church
was as important to Daddy as life itself. As a matter of
fact, death was just about the only valid excuse for
missing services. Now, he found it easier and easier
to make excuses for not going. I knew what was
going on in his mind. He had been on the other side
of the pulpit most of his life . . . this side just didn't
feel comfortable to him!

On a few occasions, we would see a faint flash of
the old "preacher" in Daddy. We would bring him to
church and at times ask him to say something to the
congregation. It was not to patronize him . . . he is
still a chosen vessel of God! At times the "anointing"
would return to him even as it did to Samson for his
final feat. Daddy would sound like the preacher he
once had been. It was hard to fight back the emotions on those occasions! We wanted him to find a
place for his ministry again, but it seemed that the
damage had already been done. He would never
return to the pulpit.

And then, he went in for surgery. During the
procedure, as I understand it, his heart stopped beating. I don't know all the details. It really doesn't matter, for I'm confident the medical personnel did everything possible. But I have wondered what lasting

effect it had on him. Did he go without oxygen to his brain too long? After that surgery, he was never the same.

Maybe it was a blessing in disguise. Now he seemed to be more at peace with his state in life. Before, I had seen him quietly fret that his denomination no longer seemed to need him. Now, he really wasn't very aware of what was going on.

As sons and daughters, we decided the best thing we could do was to comfort Mama and Daddy as the Bible says to do. For several years Mama had been in a similar condition. I'm not a doctor, so I don't know why. I suppose some of the same stresses had gotten through to her as well. Now we had the opportunity to repay a debt of love they had given to their six children.

I dare not speak words that would cause anyone to think I would bring anything but dignity to this man. My heart is broken as I watch this shell of a soldier, sitting on the porch staring into space. I wonder if it's necessary for life to be this way for him! Who is responsible? I am willing to shoulder my fair share of any blame . . . but could the Church have handled her role better?

I have heard it said that the Church is the only army that kills its wounded. Hopefully, we will increase our awareness to find solutions in effectively solving this problem. And it is not always just the old soldiers we destroy. Many times it is the young, talented soldiers whose lack of experience causes them to wander away from the true path. Mistakes made by young ministers are often fatal!

And so, I sit with my Daddy. I fight back the tears. I see him cry, and I want to cry with him. I remember him as a strong man. His voice was strong, his body was strong, and his will was strong . . . now he is like a child. He calls dozens of times a day just to hear my voice reassuring him that all is well.

Often he calls and begs to go back home to South Georgia. He doesn't realize he and Mama can't care for themselves without help. He only knows he wants to go back to his little house and his pecan trees.

I don't try to explain to him all the reasons "going home" isn't possible. I just tell him we will take him back as soon as we can work out the details. Then he looks at me with those deep blue eyes. In a small, weak voice he says, "I just want to go home."

Before long, I know we will take him home to his beloved farm. A little family graveyard there already has his marker. He will rest beneath those huge stately pecan trees in the sandy soil that beckons to him like some invisible magnet.

No, I'm not anxious to see him go there . . . yet

I know it is inevitable. I have always loved him dearly. Since I have been able to care for him, I seem to love him even more. I feel as if the responsibility he once felt to care for me has been reversed. I recall those cold mornings he saw to it that I stayed warm . . . the nights I was frightened when I stood at his bedside and he comforted me. Now when he calls me at three in the morning, I don't recoil. I simply tell him, "All is well, Daddy . . . go back to sleep."

Here he is . . . an old retired soldier in our camp, just trying to play out the string. He doesn't even have the will to fight any longer. Hopefully, we can hold his hands up for his final battle and make it a victorious one! He has indeed fought the fight and kept the faith. Henceforth, there is a crown of righteousness laid up for him which the Commander-In-Chief will personally place upon his head. If ever a man deserved a crown, Earl P. Paulk, Sr. is one such man . . . and one such soldier!

7

LAUGHTER
IS GOOD MEDICINE
– March 1985 –

I get more positive response to my humorous columns than the others. That is significant to me. It says that people want to be happy. With so much unhappiness all around us in this world, we desperately look for things to make us laugh and people to laugh with us.

I must admit that I prefer writing about pleasant things to writing about child abuse or starving children in Ethiopia. Perhaps a little escapism lives in all of us. We're aware of all the problems that face us every day, but still, we would rather laugh than cry.

What makes us laugh? The government has probably already funded a grant, commissioning research in this field. After all, they spend thousands of taxpayers dollars to find out why we snore and to explore the sex life of the tsetse fly. So why not research laughter? You will be pleased to know, however, that I have conducted my own research on the subject. I will pass my findings on to you . . . all at absolutely no cost to taxpayers and/or tithers!

First of all, we have what we call "jokes." These are more or less like socks . . . they come in all lengths and colors. Some are suitable for telling; others reflect the total depravity of man's mind. Usually, the key ingredient that makes a joke work is the unexpected. The mind is so programmed that when we listen to a joke, our mind takes a predictable path. When that path takes an unpredictable turn that we don't expect, the result is humor. Let me illustrate.

A guy is holding a cream pie. Another guy walks up to him, holding his hat in his hand. He asks the first guy to give him a piece of pie. Already, you know the guy with the pie is going to dump the cream pie in the second guy's hat. Predictable. In our mind we saw that coming and that is funny in a sort of slapstick way.

But here is the unexpected. The guy looks in his hat with pie in it and says to the first guy, "You think that's funny? Well, that's not funny. Here's funny." He then puts the hat on his own head, and with the pie running down over his ears walks away! We laugh! We didn't see that coming.

Often humor can be very cruel. Teenagers can be especially cruel to one another and think it is absolutely hilarious. Teens used to have a phrase a few years back that referred to something being as funny as a "truck load of dead babies." Obviously that is not funny, but in their way of thinking, it was. Often someone else's failure or ignorance prompts laughter. We all have a tendency to laugh at the wrong things at the wrong time.

Be honest, how many of you have ever gotten tickled at a funeral? Obviously, if the deceased is a close friend or relative, you are hard pressed to find anything humorous. But when it involves someone you really didn't know, like a friend of a friend, then watch out!

Being raised in a preacher's home, I had to attend the funerals of many people I had never seen or even heard of in my life. As children, we were bored with having to sit through these proceedings, yet we were forced to attend such occasions. We often looked for things to amuse ourselves. Do you realize that people who are grief-stricken often do exceptionally unusual things? People passing out used to be a highlight of the funerals I attended as a lad. Usually the lady who passed out was the largest and heaviest person at the service. The man who attempted to catch her was always the 90 pound weakling! Now

you gotta admit, that can be funny if you aren't bury-
ing your mama!

I recall one funeral I attended when I was about
eight years of age. At that time I was averaging about
one funeral per week. At this particular event, my dad
was the center of attention . . . literally! We arrived at
the cemetery for the interment. My dad took his place
as the presiding minister in front of the winding procession to the open grave. Mama stayed behind in the
car. Suddenly she spied something white at the rear
of Daddy's pants. She realized the whole seam had
come out of the seat of his pants. Consequently, every
step he took caused them to gap open, exposing his
white boxer shorts. Now, white shorts against the
background of a blue serge suit can be quite star-
tling, to say the least!

After her initial shock, I was quickly dispatched
on my mission—partly of mercy, partly of diplomacy,
but mostly in the interest of human decency! I
quickly went to him. I whispered a message in his ear
concerning his newest fashion-setting trend. His eye
caught mine. I could read his mind! He was saying,
"This better not be a joke, my little man." (He always
called me "my little man" when he wanted to be
stern with me!) But his examining hand quickly veri-
fied my report. I was assigned yet another mission. I
had to walk behind him as closely as possible for the

duration of the interment. Never have father and son seemed so close to one another before a congregation of mourners!

Another time when we always want to laugh and know we shouldn't is whenever someone falls down. I don't know why that is funny, but Chevy Chase made it a trademark on television. Out of decency, we usually wait until it is established whether the person is seriously injured. If only his pride has been damaged, then we laugh.

The worst place to evidence clumsiness is in church. Here, in the presence of God and our fellow worshippers, we attempt to maintain some degree of decorum. But when something occurs that breaks the mood, it can be especially disastrous!

I recall a choir member several years ago stumbling to her knees as the choir walked in procession. The carpet protected everything but her pride. I really felt sorry for her. As I looked about, I saw people trying to stifle their laughter. It was almost more than I could control. And have you ever noticed that even if we are hurt in a fall, we don't want to admit it? That in itself is funny to me!

I remember a sister of mine (who shall remain nameless), once falling to her knees on the sidewalk in front of my house. I naturally asked her if she was hurt. She laughed and said she wasn't hurt in the slightest. I looked at her knees. Her stockings were torn and both knees were bleeding profusely. Yet she insisted she wasn't hurt. I wanted to say, "Come on, Myrtle (Oops! Sorry I uncovered you, Myrt), you know your knees are stinging. Let's get something on them." But Nooo . . . she made me think she really relished pulverizing her kneecaps!

I guess in order to enjoy humor, we should first learn to laugh at ourselves. I think I am very funny . . . not that I am hilariously clever or amusing, but rather because of some of the bonehead things I do! Let me tell you what happened to me recently.

After a church service, a group of us trekked down to a local restaurant. Among the group was Gloria Copeland, wife of evangelist Kenneth Copeland, who had been with us in the services that weekend. She was catching a plane shortly, so she had to leave before everyone had finished eating. Being the southern gentleman that I am, I escorted her out to the car that was to take her to the airport.

I bade her adieu and returned to join my party. When I arrived at the front door of the restaurant, I found it was locked. We had arrived rather late and they had closed for business while our group was dining. Getting out was no problem, but now the door was locked to prevent my re-entry.

Let me further describe the situation. It was

below freezing outside. Thinking I would return in a moment, I had not worn my topcoat when I left. Bad decision! I began to beat on the door. No response. Occasionally a waitress would see me, but she merely tried to wave me away. I could see her mouth the words, "We're closed!" Thanks a bunch for that late breaking bulletin! I could see that!

I went around tapping on the windows, trying to get anyone's attention. This particular establishment is characterized by lovely stained glass windows, which of course means that no one could see the bright blue my skin was turning. Frostbite was setting in. I began to wonder what life would be like without fingers and toes.

I turned to intercessory prayer . . . "Please God, send along an unaware angel to deliver me." I started to look around for loose boards to build a fire. We non-smokers are always at a disadvantage when it comes to available fire.

Well folks, I'm here to testify that God DOES answer prayer. He DOES have a sense of humor. Surely He was getting a kick out of the whole episode. I could just see Him calling to the Apostle Peter as He watched me darting around in my clerical attire. "Hey Pete, I have a riddle! What is black and white and blue all over?"

I could picture them having a heavenly laugh at

mortal futility. Finally, He decided to send help just before I became the Abominable Snowman. But even then, there was a humorous little twist. He sent my son, Donnie Earl. My son finds everything funny, apparently even his father at the door of death! Already I am getting sleepy . . . isn't that the way they say you freeze to death?

Donnie Earl had decided to come to the phone in the entrance way. I had, in my hour of despair, made several promises to God. The past few minutes had seemed like an eternity. Why hasn't Clariece missed me? I could just see her inside laughing, having the time of her life while my body froze as stiff as a carp! One thing I did promise God, however, was to be very grateful to any rescuer He would send.

I pounded on the door and got Donnie Earl's attention. He took one look at me and laughed! "Since when are icicles on your father's nose funny?" I thought. My first thought was to place my hands around his neck and let him experience the grip of a man who has just been frozen alive!

Suddenly, not only did I remember my sacred promise to be nice to my rescuer, but the whole thing struck me funny also. Through partially frozen lips I laughed at my predicament . . . one I had brought upon myself.

I think we take ourselves far too seriously most

of the time. I want to see humor in life. I am not talking about the inability to be serious or comprehend weighty issues. If we don't learn to laugh at ourselves and with others, we may well find out that life has become stale, stagnant and perhaps meaningless.

When I need a good laugh, I have learned where I can always find one. I just watch other preachers . . . especially the pompous ones who still think it is a mortal sin to smile. I picture them standing before their congregations when they suddenly realize they have forgotten to dress. They are behind the pulpit without any clothes on! Maybe it's a little bit like the story of *The Emperor's New Clothes*. Remember that story? Now, there's a story almost too close to home to laugh about . . .

8

LOVE MEANS SAYING I'M SORRY
– November 1985 –

Donnie Earl and his dad

Donnie Earl 1987

Donnie Earl #77

Being a father can be extremely frustrating . . . being a father who happens to be a pastor can be especially frustrating. It seems preachers are supposed to have attained some degree of perfection in life. I have always endeavored to be a good father, but many times I show that I, too, am merely mortal. I guess one of the most difficult things any parent must do, regardless of his title, is allow his children to grow up and live their own lives. We start off doing everything for them. Then it's often difficult to find the appropriate quitting place!

Our responsibility is to lay strong foundations for our children to attain their highest potential and become the unique individuals God purposed them to be. They are not simply extensions of our own egos. However, if we are not cautious, we find ourselves trying to hitch a ride on our children's intimate personal journeys.

This particular topic has become very real to me in the past few months. LaDonna is twenty years old and hopefully the training her mother and I have given her will be manifested in the life she lives and the decisions she makes. No longer am I able to make choices for her. Now I must stand aside and watch her be her own person in the world and in the eyes of God. My present and continuing function in her life now is supplying advice and friendship, coupled with an abundance of love and prayer.

Donnie Earl, however, is another story! He is twelve years old and still in those very volatile and formative years. These past twelve years have brought with them my discovery of the vast difference between raising a boy and raising a girl. A girl will pretty much take you at your word and accept verbal correction. But with a boy, you have to teach him the way more emphatically! Perhaps it is the male instinct that is beginning to stir within. Usually the "end" result is that he requires more "hands on" instruction!

Perhaps it is natural for a father to want to live out his own fantasies through his son, however good his intentions. Basically, I think a father wants his son to be better and do better in everything than he did. But there is a fine line we must not cross. Otherwise, we find ourselves vicariously and even dangerously trying to live their lives for them.

I found this to be painfully true this year when Donnie Earl played football. Unfortunately, I was reared in a church that believed playing any type of ball was inherently sinful. I wanted to play so badly, but because of the religious convictions of my family, I was not allowed to participate. Therefore, when the opportunity presented itself for me to play anyplace . . . the street, the sandlot, a pick-up game, I always took full advantage.

I always had this obsession about never allowing anyone to outrun me . . . and few ever did! What I lacked in size, I compensated for with speed and desire. When I did get to a denominational school where I could play ball (there had been some relaxation of the discipline of the church), I threw myself into the fray with total abandonment! I played tailback in a single wing formation. That will tell you football buffs about how old I am! (Methuselah was my fullback!)

The years of deprivation unleashed an onslaught of incredible intensity into my playing style. It's not that I ever wanted to hurt anyone, but when I played defense (we also played two-ways!), I definitely sought to establish my presence in the mind of my opponent! I never really knew how good or bad I could have been because of the religious restrictions imposed upon me earlier in life. One university did contact me during college because of my speed. I didn't want to create problems within my family and church, so I passed it up. I promised myself right then and there, I would never prevent my kids from participating in athletics because of some doctrinal dogma. It almost caused me to resent God at one point in my life. I vowed never to force a son to play ball, but if he chose to play, I would certainly encourage him in every way.

I can see that Donnie Earl has some innate athletic ability. In all probability, he will be larger and stronger than I am at his "P.R.G." (present rate of growth). I am convinced that it's inherent for me to want to see him develop his skills and be the best he can be.

But in retrospect, I realize that I had begun to push him. I found myself "coaching" him on our drives home from school and delivering some pretty scathing critiques of his performances at practice. "Why did you let that running back get outside?" "Why didn't you pressure the quarterback?" "Why walk down the field rather than run?" I covered every facet of his game!

And then one afternoon as we were driving home and I was pulling my Knute Rockne act, I saw his head turn away from me toward the window. I caught the glint of a tear on his cheek. I felt as if a hammer had struck me between the eyes and I had been kicked in the stomach at the same time! I realized instantly what was happening! It was no longer merely a game. I had taken all the fun out of it for him. No longer was I a supportive father . . . I had become just another coach hollering at him!

Through the years I had watched other parents do the same thing in little league. I had purposed never to repeat any of their critical ways. Now as I reflected on my careless and inconsiderate actions, I saw how I had stood on the sidelines giving him "thumbs down" signs for every missed tackle or at least what "I" felt was sloppy play. I never screamed like some other parents would do, but in my own subtle way, I made my displeasure known to Donnie Earl.

Now the sight of that single tear on his cheek stood as an indictment against my thoughtlessness. I realized that I had sadly become something I so totally abhorred as I attempted to live out my fantasies at the expense of my child.

I drove along quietly, trying to decide what to say. I glanced over and saw his head still turned toward the window. He is at the age he doesn't want people to see him cry. So quickly he is becoming a man, yet still housed inside that growing body is a little boy that can be hurt so deeply. I knew that what I said now might make the difference in our future relationship.

I have seen parents who feel it is important for their children to be taught that they are always right . . . perfect, never making a mistake. I have actually heard parents say to their children, "Even if I'm wrong, I'm right!" And then, when that child eventually discovers the parent is only mortal, it often brings bitter disillusionment. I want always to have credibility with my children. They must realize that I am doing the best I can to make the right decisions. I am not perfect. I fully accept the risk of making mistakes. After all, no school exists where one can learn the rules of being a "perfect father." Experience is the only teacher, and I've been their dad the exact same amount of time they've been my children . . . so my "on the job training" is somewhat limited and certainly far from faultless.

I had made a mistake. I knew the right thing was to admit it, not only to myself, but also to Donnie Earl as well. I started to speak . . . it was difficult. It's not that I was too proud to admit to my son that I had been wrong. I just desperately wanted to say the right thing. I wanted to maintain his respect for me, making our bond of love even stronger than ever before.

At last I said to him that I realized I had forgotten a promise I had made to myself. I had promised never to push him into anything that was possibly motivated by my own ego or in any way was influenced by my past experiences. I admitted that I was only human. Therefore, the very real probability existed that this would not be the last error I would ever make. I promised him that I would always be willing to tell him when I had said or done the wrong thing. I would try to correct my mistakes.

I think we both learned a very valuable lesson that day. He learned that I was mortal and could be wrong. But hopefully, he also learned that I would be fair. Most of all, he knew that I loved him more than I could ever express. I pray for him to understand. I hope he realizes that my mistakes are honest ones, committed by an overzealous father who only wants the very best for his son.

And I learned again the importance of being sensitive to my children. They all too soon learn to cover up their emotions . . . they don't want us to see them cry. (I wonder where they learned that?) Do you remember a song that came out a few years back entitled, *Don't Let The Sun Catch You Cryin'*? I was just thinking that it might be better titled, *Go Ahead, Let the Sun Catch You Cryin'*, or how about this version . . . *It's All Right Dad, to Let Your Son Catch You Cryin'*! A tear on the cheek, quietly wiped away, can speak a significantly important message to us. Let's not ever stop listening . . . or crying . . . I pray I don't . . .

9

THE BIRTH OF PUPPIES
– February 1982 –

Pastor Don and friends

Some readers are concerned that I don't write on more "spiritual" subject matter. Apparently, some people don't think writing is spiritual unless it (a) quotes a multiplicity of scriptures; (b) talks about sin and how God is going to vent His wrath on sinners; (c) uses obvious spiritual sounding phrases such as "in my spirit I feel . . ." (which by the way has become one of the most trite phrases used regularly in the religious world!)

However, I believe that life itself is a tremendously "spiritual" experience. Indeed, God is the Creator and Giver of life. What can be more "spiritual" than God Himself? Hidden away in our God-given lives are spiritual truths. Readers will just have to search for truths among all the verbiage that I write. For those who think in "spiritual" and in "non-spiritual" terms, here is a column written on what some may perceive to be a thoroughly "non-spiritual" subject! But here goes . . .

About a year ago someone left three furry little puppies in a cardboard box on the parking lot of our church. Obviously the anonymous donor had heard about a resident "soft touch" pastor here! I tried desperately to find homes for these three little orphaned puppies due to the fact that I already had a large dog at home to support. I located homes for two of them right away. That still left one little lady, shivering and shaking as she huddled in the corner of the box. She looked into my face, seemingly asking, "Are you my mother?"

Donnie Earl's birthday was just around the corner. I decided a puppy would make a great gift for him. In my moment of passion and great benevolence, I overlooked the fact that this small furry creature with the black button eyes would all too soon grow up to be an adult dog. Furthermore, being on the distaff side, she could potentially be a mother dog sometime in the near future.

And that is exactly what happened . . . she quickly became an adult dog. Though she was not a large animal, she was fully capable of all maternal rights inherent to the female of any species! We christened her "Lady," which though not exactly a unique moniker, hopefully bespoke her character.

At this point in time, there already abode another canine at our address, she also being of questionable lineage. You see, God apparently instilled in stray and homeless dogs a homing device which directs them straight to me. But because she was indeed a "she," I figured we had no great problem maintaining the dog population at my house to two (2)! Right?

Wrong! Enter one large, mostly white, male dog who obviously could also boast of combining several breeds in his bloodline. Now, we needed another dog like we needed more fleas! But here he was . . . homeless and with those big, sad, brown eyes. He stayed! First, we had to give him a name. So far, he answered to anything we called him! He would have responded to "Daisy," just as long as we would feed him. We assigned Donnie Earl with selecting a name for this new addition to our growing kennel. He couldn't settle on one, so he provided us with two names. The dog soon answered to either "Butch" or "Bruno."

Being a father and a relatively well-versed man in animal husbandry, I realized a potentially danger-ous situation was developing here which could possi-bly result in the sudden increase of our canine population.

One small female dog plus one large male dog equals big trouble! As one of my favorite scriptures says, "that which I have feared most has come upon me." (And some people say I never use scripture references!)

And it did indeed come upon me. As Lady began to expand her borders, I realized that in approximately 57 to 63 days one or more blessed events would emerge at our house.

As you might have guessed, Lady's hour of deliverance came on a Saturday night. If anything is ever going to go wrong in a preacher's house, it will be that night! It is a diabolical plot of Satan to unsettle you before Sunday!

Having served as a "mid-husband" at other canine deliveries, I recognized that the moment of truth was imminent. I made the necessary preparations. Lady and I joined together in a moment of prayer, threw in some "Hail Marys" just for good measure, and embarked upon that wondrous and mystical phenomenon of seeing new life burst forth!

Clariece passed through where I had temporarily set up my MASH unit and eyed me with some degree of skepticism. I read her look which said, "I told you if you let that dog stay here, this would happen." I decided rather than defend my compassion for homeless animals, I would disarm her with humor. I quipped, "Lawzy, Miss Scarlett. I don't know nuthin' 'bout birthin' puppies." Her stern stare informed me that my sad attempt at humor had not assuaged her growing irritability. Thankfully, she scurried away to other important missions in life.

At precisely 6:05 a.m. EST (I wanted to accurately document this historic event!) Lady began to bear the fruit of her previous indiscretion and my negligence. I suppose I should have sat her down and explained the birds and the bees . . . and large white dogs!

Let me emphasize here that Bruno/Butch was a large dog and Lady was a small dog. For the next nine hours that little dog labored diligently to give birth to six . . . count em' . . . LARGE, healthy puppies. However, what we experienced was more than a deliverance of sextuplets. We had a genuine population explosion! And when it was over, we were all "dog tired!"

I sat by reverently watching this new mother attend her newborn. Again, I marvelled at the miracle of birth. I watched this exhausted little female dog, once just a scrubby orphan in a cardboard box, instinctively perform a task that only an infinite God could instill within her. She had never attended any LaMaze classes, had never read any books, nor heard

any panel discussions . . . yet, she knew exactly what
to do! She had become an instant mother!

During this whole ordeal, Donnie Earl was my
one semi-faithful assistant. He sized up the situation
and decided to witness only those portions of the
proceedings that interested him. Even though his
spirit was willing, his flesh occasionally grew squeam-
ish! (Hey, another scriptural reference!)

Now folks, I realize I haven't expounded on the
five-fold ministry or those things that may appear to
be obviously "spiritual," but look very carefully
in this little story and see a dimension of true
spirituality.

Spirituality is a state of being . . . not merely
rituals or liturgies, nor even pious sounding plati-
tudes. A man can indeed be "spiritual" by repairing
his kid's bike or by doing something that will build a
close relationship between a father and his child;
Sometimes "spiritual" may be as simple as befriend-
ing an orphaned mongrel.

So, the next time you want to be "spiritual,"
remember that God asks us, "Doesn't nature teach
you . . .?" Yes, we can learn many lessons from
nature. Whether witnessing the birth of a puppy or
viewing a magnificent crimson sky at sunset, the
most ordinary experience can be transformed into the
extraordinary. The most common dwelling can become

a sacred cathedral . . . if we only take the time to see
. . . if we only take the time . . .

10

A SENTIMENTAL JOURNEY
– April 1982 –

Daddy, Mama, Sister Myrtle, me and twin sister Darlene

Soldier Don, WWII

Twins Darlene and Don

One day I just needed to be alone to think some things through and sort them out. I began driving on the expressway with no particular destination in mind. The solitude of the car provided a quiet refuge for the moment, away from adverse circumstances that had created turmoil around me. I found myself driving north. A couple of hours later I saw a sign that read "Next Exit Greenville." Before I realized it, I had driven to Greenville, South Carolina, which incidentally is the place of my birth.

I had not intended to drive this far. Perhaps, even for some subconscious reason, I had been drawn back to the place where I started my earthly pilgrimage. I'm sure everyone has those special places that are a part of childhood memories . . . places they associate with their unharried days of youth. Greenville is one such city for me. It is the southern reserve that holds my most pleasant childhood memories.

Certain locations and scenes repeatedly reappear in my dreams . . . the house I lived in when I began school . . . the street where I lived . . . the school I attended . . . the church my dad pastored . . . even the very house in which I was born. (It was not unusual in 1938 for a child to be born at home.)

Since I had already come this far, I decided to take the Greenville exit and call on some of those friendly memories of the past. I found myself on Augusta Road, a very familiar road to me. The house where I had lived and the school I had attended were only a couple of blocks off this major Greenville thoroughfare.

I drove to 107 Elm Street, an address forever etched in my mind. I lived here when I started the first grade. I pulled the car to the curb in front of the house. I sat there looking at a familiar, yet strangely unfamiliar sight.

The whole scene was much smaller than I had remembered it. I remembered Elm street as a wide boulevard. Now I realized it was actually just a little, ordinary, narrow street, obviously built before two and three cars were part of the average family. It was lined with large trees and comfortable mid-sized homes which sat much closer to each other than I had envisioned.

Fixed in my mind were memories of a yard that had been the size of a football field. That remembrance is probably due to the fact here I first cut grass with an antiquated push-mower. I could close my eyes and almost smell the green pungency of a freshly-mowed lawn. And yet now it all seemed like a yellowed, miniature-sized photograph from some old attic postcard.

I looked down at the sidewalk where we played "snake in the gully" for hours. I had learned how to ride a bike on this very sidewalk . . . a J.C. Higgin's blue beauty from Sears and Roebuck. I had spilled what seemed like pints of blood on this stretch of concrete—skinned elbows, knees and toes. Though the years had long since washed the adolescent blood stains away, the memories indelibly lingered on.

I saw a man open the front door of the red brick house and cross the porch where I had played so many times. He came down the steps and walked down the sidewalk. I got out of my car and started toward him, wanting to intercept his destination. I quickly proceeded to explain that I had lived in this house in 1943 and wondered if I might possibly look around a bit. With his permission I continued my "sentimental journey."

I strolled down the driveway toward the back of the house. It had been built in days when garages were constructed separately from the house. That white frame garage still stood there like a silent sentinel. It had always protected the gleaming black Pontiac my dad used to drive.

In the corner of the yard, I noticed the pecan tree that my dad and I had planted with our own hands. I had personally supplied many gallons of water from my bucket for its thirsty roots. Now it was a huge tree.

Still strung across the yard from the house out to the garage was a power line that had once been severed by my errant football! In another corner of the backyard I searched to find a stately willow tree that we had also planted. I was saddened to see that it was gone. A peep into a basement window revealed that the old coal burning furnace I had stoked so often was now replaced by a more modern piece of equipment.

I looked at the neighboring houses. The sight evoked visions of other days and other sounds. There were voices of children at play . . . Jimmy Carrol, Tommy Morgan, Clyde White, and Lynn, a curly haired little girl whose last name I couldn't remember. She had been one of my first "patients" when I practiced "medicine" during my short-lived medical career which ended abruptly at age six when some adult stumbled onto our "clinic"!

Donaldson Elementary School was no longer there. The huge swings that once adorned its play yard are now replaced by a modern office building, complete with its own version of swings and erector sets. It was sort of sad. I remembered that old school as a building with great character and charm. Its ornate frontispiece came to mind . . . I recall how mammoth it appeared to me when I walked through that huge door the first day of school. I wondered if one of the young minds trained at Donaldson Elementary was in any way responsible for the "progress" that now stood in the form of a nondescript glass and metal building, looking rather out of place under the mighty old Donaldson oak trees.

I drove away from that site with a feeling of melancholy. I remembered the phrase Thomas Wolfe said . . . "you can never go home again." I passed Jones Mortuary where the old horse-drawn hearse was still on display in the front yard. I wondered where their daughter, Loy, was. I hadn't seen her in thirty-nine years.

Slowly, I drove on to the church my dad had pastored. As a matter of fact, he had built the church. In those days it was considered to be one of the largest Pentecostal churches in the whole country. I got out and walked to the cornerstone and read the inscription: ERECTED 1948. REV. EARL P. PAULK, SR., PASTOR. Even though the wording was redundant, it so reminded me of my dad. In those days he had been a strong man about my present age. To me he was the strongest man who ever lived. He was also the wisest man in the world, a man who could run the fastest and preach the best.

The cornerstone further read, "To Be Opened in the Year 2000." My dad, along with many others, had placed a New Testament inside the cornerstone. In the year 2000 these Bibles, along with other items, will be given to the nearest living relative. I stood and looked at this church, a marvel when it was first erected. It had replaced a church that had been gutted by fire. As it had burned, hundreds of members in the neighborhood gathered and cried as they watched their spiritual home disappear in flames. My dad had resolved to build them the most beautiful church possible. He kept his promise. To him, this was the most gorgeous building ever constructed!

I stood with all these memories rushing through my mind . . . I remembered Mama, such a beautiful woman. I loved to come home from school in the afternoons and smell her pinto beans cooking. To this day, when I recognize the aroma of pinto beans, again I am a ten year old boy!

I didn't realize that for the past couple of hours I had been translated back to another time, another era. I had forgotten my problems which piled up this particular day. I didn't understand exactly how it had happened. All the things that had been on my mind, strangely enough, began to sort themselves out. I had a new perspective. Now they really didn't seem that big after all!

Time is indeed a healer. Today's crisis is tomorrow's memory. The cares of life will certainly pass, even as the years go by. All of a sudden, I felt like going home again.

I thought of LaDonna and Donnie Earl. They now are in the process of making contributions to their own collection of memories. Thirty-five years from now, what will they call to mind? As they reflect on their pasts, what will be their remembrances of home and of me . . . their father? I stopped at a telephone booth and dialed my number. I told Clariece I would be home in a couple of hours.

LaDonna found out I was on the other end of the line. I heard the sound of her voice. She didn't have to say very much. She softly said only what I really needed to hear, "Daddy, I love you." I cranked the engine and headed back down Augusta Road toward home . . .

11

OKEFENOKEE TRIP
– February 1981 –

Father and son team

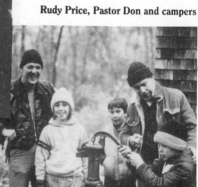

Rudy Price, Pastor Don and campers

The Whole Group

The Flotilla

When they first began talking about getting up a trip to the Okefenokee Swamp, I should have run in the opposite direction as quickly as my legs could carry me. But no! I entertained the idea, letting it play around in my mind a little bit, actually dabbling with the thought of going.

You see, I can't feign total ignorance of The Big "O". . . the largest swamp in the United States. Both my parents were born and raised within fifty miles of this wonder of nature. I spent enough summers and other days there to know basically what kind of conditions we're talking about. I had been to Big Creek, Sweetwater Creek, the Altamaha River swamp, Fargo and Ludowici enough times to know what a swamp is like. And like the sea that lures unsuspecting sailors away, I began listening to the call of the swamp.

Anyway, I didn't want all those other guys in the church to think I was soft! And besides, wouldn't this make a great trip for a dad and his eight year old son? Just the two of us away in the wilderness, roughing it!

And so in the month of January, which is not a month for any civilized outdoor activity, seventeen foolhardy souls packed our gear and headed south for Great Adventure! Among us were mostly adult men, one woman, a couple of almost grown girls, and three younger boys, my Donnie Earl being the youngest.

We arrived at the swamp after dark. We decided to camp overnight in a public camp area and wait until daylight to make our grand entrance into the Big "O." I should have known I was in serious trouble when I almost froze to death during the night. And this was in spite of (1) long johns, (2) jeans, (3) a flannel shirt, (4) insulated coveralls, (5) a heavy coat, (6) fleece-lined gloves, (7) a stocking cap pulled entirely over my whole head like a ski mask, and (8) a single sleeping bag with both me and Donnie Earl huddled together for body warmth!

There was an air of expectancy the next morning, especially among the kids. But somewhere in the back of my mind I had this gnawing feeling that I had chosen to do the wrong thing! Fate was just

about to do a number on me! I could already antici-
pate my impending destiny. Maybe I would lose a leg
to an alligator or be bitten by a cottonmouth moc-
casin. Well, it was too late to turn back now. I considered my options. I could feign illness or make a quick
call back to Atlanta and need to make an "emergency" trip back home. Or I could just balk like an
old stubborn mule and say, "I ain't goin' in that devil
swamp!" As I watched Donnie Earl darting about
excitedly, all my options vanished. I had to go
through with this for his sake. I didn't want him to
look at me years from now and accuse me of being a
wimp!

It is quite amazing how certain events surface
"experts" among us! It's been said that an expert is
anyone further than one hundred miles from his own
home. Everyone on this trip qualified! Among us were
insurance salesmen, airline pilots, home builders,
computer reps, swimming pool managers and even
one librarian! (Shush!) And now suddenly, everyone
was a veteran "outdoorsperson." (I use that home-
made term in deference to the female persons among
us!)

Almost instantly our "experts" were at a variance
of opinions! Some contended we had to paddle six-
teen miles to our destination, while others main-
tained it was only fourteen miles. It made no differ-

ence to me . . . once I had heard the general figure, I went into semi-shock! Me . . . paddle a canoe 14-16 miles? In one day? My gnawing fears were no longer slight . . . very quickly they had grown to a voracious paranoia of impending doom. By this time I was just trying to keep a low profile so that the others, particularly Donnie Earl, wouldn't read the fear in my face! We all paired off into two man canoes. My partner obviously was my eight year old son. Now it doesn't take a genius to figure out that the canoes manned by two able-bodied adult males are going to have an easier time than one canoe bearing one middle-aged, under-exercised man with an eight-year-old boy whose main activity was shifting his weight precariously from one place to the other!

The trip began with all the canoes strung out single file in the marked channels that wind deeper and deeper into what the Indians called the "land of trembling earth." Our canoe was somewhere about midway in the flotilla. What I had hoped would be a leisurely trip down the scenic channels quickly degraded into a race towards our destination, Floyd's Island, right in the center of the swamp. I tried to keep pace. I wondered how I could have been so cold last night and now be sweating so profusely.

Along the channel there were mile markers. Upon realizing we needed to paddle 14-16 miles (depending upon which "expert's" information you chose to believe!), the sign of "mile one" was not very encouraging, especially when one is already fighting to maintain consciousness from exhaustion! I had already seen all of the swamp I cared to see! Actually, I had seen MORE than I cared to see!

We were facing a fairly stiff breeze. When paddling into a wind, a condition is created known to physicists as the "sucking air feeling like you're gonna die" syndrome! The wind kept pushing us into the tall marsh grass and muddy bogs . . . everywhere but the marked channels.

At the "mile eight" sign, our first tragedy struck. As I said, the whole thing had degenerated into a wild race with the canoe behind us hard on our stern, challenging us for our position. I used to like to race when I was young. At this stage in life, the killer instinct has subsided considerably. I am perfectly content to watch others wear themselves out for the privilege of arriving at the finish line first. But little Donnie Earl had the spirit of competition and began begging, "Come on, Dad, don't let them pass us."

Greater love hath no man than to tax his body for a pleading son! I poured on the steam, but two able-bodied seamen were neck and neck with us! The channel was narrow and not really designed to accommodate two canoes side by side. One of the contestants in the other canoe then took his paddle and placed it against our canoe, pushing us toward the bank. Blatant Sabotage!

Being in the front of the canoe, Donnie Earl was the first to arrive at the scene of the accident! There were overhanging dense bushes into which he went headlong. When I extracted our vessel from the brush, I surveyed the damage. A limb had torn a hole in Donnie Earl's lip. Blood was all over his mouth! Time to panic! Time to pray! Time to pray a panicky prayer!

"I must gain control of this situation," I thought to myself. "Here we are in the middle of a swamp! God, where are You? I don't relish the sight of blood, and especially on the face of my son in the middle of the Okefenokee Swamp!" I tried to think more clearly. Where is the first aid kit? I recalled them saying we had one. I secretly hoped it also included a surgeon who could do stitches!

I remembered then that the first aid kit was in the canoe ahead of us. Bear in mind, I have already explained that this whole thing had become a race to Floyd's Island or death . . . whichever came first! I began to heave-to in order to catch the canoe with the first aid kit. Our librarian and part-time crossing guard was the captain of that vessel . . . she is a very competitive person. (As a matter of fact, SHE won the race over all the other able-bodied adult male contestants!) Suffice it to say, when she saw me coming at a high rate of speed, she erroneously concluded I was seeking to challenge the navigational skills she was exhibiting in her two "person" canoe! Subsequently, she demonstrated her mastery of the art of paddling and pulled further away. She left me behind in the wake of an emotional frenzy along with some other feelings I dare not describe here!

Donnie Earl was the only cool one aboard! "It's alright, Dad. No problem." Sure kid, that's easy for you to say. You are only bleeding to death. You will soon be out of your misery, but I have to return home to face a distraught mother with your little emaciated body! Now there's a fate WORSE than death!

When I realized I couldn't catch the "good ship lollipop" which had been transformed into the world's fastest oar-operated speed boat, I could only pray. Folks, miracles do still happen! God answered my prayer . . . the bleeding had almost stopped. I liberally thanked God, but implored Him to remain on standby. I had the feeling this ordeal wasn't over yet. As they say, "It ain't over 'til the fat lady sings!"

About dusk we arrived at Floyd's Island. The race was over. I quickly informed the proud winner that I had tried to overtake her craft for medicinal purposes only. (At least I could put her on a guilt trip!)

After you have seen Floyd's Island, you wonder why you risked life and limb to paddle 14-16 miles to see this marvel of nature! Granted, if you get excited over Spanish moss, cypress trees, mud and lily pads, then you will be ecstatic! Otherwise, you have only survived the first half of a course in self-destruction!

Perhaps it was the emotional trauma of the day's events or the over-exertion of my body, but I began to feel very nauseated. It is important for you to understand something about me which I hope I can explain very tastefully . . . when I get sick, I GET SICK! When I get sick at my house, everyone else usually gets sick along with me just from hearing me get sick. That is sick!

And furthermore, when I am sick, the last thing I want to smell is food. And of all the food I don't want to smell, it is popcorn. And right then on Floyd's Island it was . . . you guessed it . . . supper time! And do you know what was on the menu? Right! Popcorn!

At this point I decided to conduct a private excursion of the island. I left my "souvenirs" and staggered back to the cabin. I collapsed on a sleeping bag and silently prayed a two part prayer: (a) God, let me die! (b) God, don't let me die!

Since I have been sick before and did survive, I

hoped "this too shall pass" eventually. But hark! What was happening to me? Something very strange was going on with my heart. It didn't feel like it was beating . . . it felt as if it were only fluttering! "My God," I prayed, "I'm having heart failure here in the middle of nowhere!"

I felt faint as if I were going to fall. I thought to myself, "I can't fall . . . I'm lying down. You can't fall up!"

More prayer. Intense prayer. Promises. Vows. I reviewed my life as it passed before my eyes. I lapsed in and out of a comatose state. "God, are You there? Remember, I asked You to standby! Okay, God, let's strike a bargain. You give me 24 hours to get my kid out of here, and then I promise I'll go quietly. Just don't let him see his dad die in the wilderness." God put me on hold . . . said He'd get back to me later. "Enjoy your misery. Maybe you'll learn a lesson or two."

Events of the night all ran together after that. A mouse openly played in the room, foraging our gear for a snack, and there was either a bear or a raccoon on the porch going through our foodstuff. No one was brave enough to open the door to see which it was. Whatever it was, it could drag a big ice cooler across the porch!

We told stories as campers like to do around

campfires. Someone suggested we all tell the most embarrassing thing that had ever happened to us. One guy told about feeling of some woman's knee under a table, thinking it was his wife's. Even in my delirious state, I didn't believe that story!

However, I KNEW that the most embarrassing moment in my life was about to occur. It would take place tomorrow, but I wouldn't be alive to enjoy it! It would be when they tied a rope to my stiff body and floated me out of the swamp like a fallen log! You see, no one comes looking for you until it's too late. That's the way it works here. When you enter the swamp, you check in with the Ranger and tell him when you are coming out. He then waits 'til you are supposed to be out. If you don't show up by that time, he organizes a search party and rides in looking for you. By then, rigor mortis has set in and you no longer fit into a canoe, hence they tie a rope to you and float you out! And THAT is to be my most embarrassing moment!

Thus pondering my demise, I lay there, suspended between life and death. I must have died. There was calm . . . and peace . . . and silence . . . total serenity. My eyes opened. Is this heaven? If so, why is there a Coleman lantern hanging here? Hallelujah, I am alive . . . I am happy!

Just when my happiness was beginning to register, it simultaneously dawned on me that I had to paddle back OUT 14-16 miles! "On second thought, Lord, just take me on with You now." The answer was apparently "No!" It seems that saints had interceded in my behalf back home. So it WASN'T my prayers that got His attention! That's just what I needed to go along with my spirit of rejection! He bypassed my prayers and went right for answering the heavyweights! Thanks a bunch! I'll remember that the next time I die!

"Okay, Lord, I'll go back home, but only if You will allow me one more little request. Could I have just a little help on the way out? I noticed on the way in that Wayne Slappey is pretty good with the paddle. Could you loan him to me?"

I would have asked for the librarian, but I couldn't have lived with myself if I had to admit that I had been rescued from the swamp by a woman! Not that I am a male chauvinist . . . but she had already beaten us all to the island! It was going to take us years to live that down!

"Maybe I could just attach a small line to Wayne's boat and he could provide enough help to get me out . . . maybe I could salvage a little self-respect in the eyes of my son! I CAN? Thanks, God! I won't forget this!"

At either the "mile eight" or "mile ten" sign,

(depending on which expert's information you chose to believe) another minor miracle occurred. A fellow boater, one with an actual outboard motor attached, appeared in the channel. Yes, he understood our dilemma. He knew there was a very sick man present. And yes, he would take us in tow and ferry us to safety! God bless him! God bless America! The hostage had been released! Apple Pie! A Coke with ice in it! Home! A mother and her whole son reunited! God is not dead!

I assume other trips will be planned. Other people will troop off into the wilderness to challenge their wits against nature. But unless God deals with me specifically, I won't be one of those troopers! As a matter of fact, the next time I feel like roughing it, I have already decided what I will do. I will take off my collar and put on a short-sleeved shirt and check in at a Holiday Inn. Now that's more like it . . .

12

THE MILK OF
HUMAN KINDNESS
– November 1984 –

Animal lover Clariece

Brother Earl, Jr and friends

I often wonder if the milk of human kindness has clabbered! Man's inhumanity to his fellow man is a spectre that utterly astounds me! It is often difficult to comprehend the lengths one human will go to make another one miserable.

Being a "people watcher," I have discovered some insights by observation. I watch to see how people treat dumb or helpless animals. Now, I understand that not everyone is an avowed animal lover as I may be. Not everyone owns or even should own a pet. But to me, it is significant when a person goes out of his way to abuse animals.

One of the last fights I had as a boy was defending a cat against several boys who were tossing it high into the air. They wanted to see if indeed it would land on its feet. As a result of their "experiment," the cat was killed. They thought it was funny. I was enraged!

I believe a person who mistreats an innocent animal will also mistreat a fellow human being under certain conditions. I have been accused of being a "softie" where animals are concerned. I would rather bear that label than to be callous, cruel or brutal to any of God's creatures.

I often use animals to teach lessons to my children. Recently, my brother Earl called me with this story after returning from a nearby tennis court. As he was leaving the courts, he saw a mother dog with a small puppy which someone had obviously abandoned at these rural courts. He had tried to call the mother to him, but because of her fear and protectiveness over her puppy, she wouldn't come. He realized it would probably take two people to render any type of assistance to her.

And he just happened to KNOW the two people who could come to the rescue! On the phone he told me of her furtive black eyes as she stood her ground between him and the puppy. He casually mentioned where she was. He didn't suggest I do anything. He just planted the seed and gave me the information in an "inadverdent" manner! I fell hook, line and sinker for the challenge!

I picked Donnie Earl up from school and we drove to the tennis courts. He asked where we were going, and I told him about the story his Uncle Earl had told me. We were going to see if we could rescue the puppy. He was all ready for the project! That pleased me. When I see compassion in him toward animals, I know that quality can easily be transferred to concern and love for people.

When we arrived at the scene, we found her just as she had been described. She was a small "Benji" type dog, standing guard in the middle of the road. I knew her puppy was nearby. As we came around the curve, she darted into some underbrush. We parked the truck and started walking slowly toward the place where she had disappeared into the bushes. As we got closer, we were greeted by low, moaning growls. I have raised enough dogs to understand what different growls mean. This was a serious growl! It meant she would fight to the death if necessary to defend her young!

I instructed Donnie Earl to talk to her calmly in a pleasant voice. You can say cruel things to a dog, but if you say them in a pleasant voice, he will think you are being kind! Dogs listen to voice intonations and inflections, not the words.

We surveyed the situation and realized we needed some tools for this mission. First, we needed

some food to entice the dog. We went to McDonald's
and bought a hamburger. When we returned, we
threw small bits of hamburger near the mother dog.
We could see her dark eyes in the bushes, and an
occasional glint of white bared fangs whenever we
ventured too close.

We had to be patient. We waited for her to smell
the food. I knew she must be hungry, for she probably
had been forced to forage for food for days. Finally,
her hunger pains prevailed. She began to slip closer
to the food. After she had eaten what we had tossed
her, we threw more bits of food, but this time, further
away from her puppy. Little by little she moved
further away from the little puppy who was huddled
back in the bushes, trembling in fear.

As I distracted her and kept her moving further
away, Donnie Earl was on his stomach, inching his
way toward the puppy. At last he grasped it. Quickly
he darted to the safety of the truck with the puppy.
As soon as the door closed, the mother instinctively
knew she had been outwitted. She dashed back to
where she had left her puppy. Finding it gone, she
began circling around, looking frantically for it.

The puppy had been my first concern. Now I
realized I couldn't drive away and leave a distraught
mother behind. But how could we put this dog into a
truck with us? Only moments earlier she had been

ready to attack us with bared fangs! This maneuver
called for strategy!

I took the puppy in my hand and slowly
approached the mother dog. She eyed me suspi-
ciously as she retreated into the underbrush. I could
sense her trying to develop her own strategy! How
could she recover her puppy from me? She watched
me intently, her dark eyes following every move I
made. Her intensity made me prepare to drop the
puppy and run if she charged!

I squatted down, placed the puppy on the
ground and began to stroke it. I talked to it sooth-
ingly. As I talked to the puppy, I looked at the mother
and included her in my conversation. "I'm not going
to hurt your puppy. Come on and let me pet you. I
won't hurt you." Slowly, she inched her way closer.
When she was only a few feet away, I took the puppy
in my hands and stood up while continuing to talk
gently to her.

She repeatedly retreated a few feet, and then
came back toward me and her puppy. She was playing
the game my way. She sensed I held all the cards in
my hand at the moment! Then she came close to me
and raised up on her hind legs to look in my hands to
see if it were still alright. I assured her it was.

Her belligerence was fading. She had seen that I
wasn't harming her puppy. I was beginning to make

her understand that I didn't want to harm her either. I could tell she had been kicked so often that she feared I would scream at her and kick her at any moment. She didn't know how to deal with this new human attitude toward her!

I held the puppy where she could sniff it and see that it was alright, all the while backing toward my truck. I softly told Donnie Earl to open the door. As he did, I gently laid the puppy in the floorboard. Then I stood aside and talked to the mother, coaxing her to get in and see her puppy. She came haltingly, but little by little she moved toward us. She seemed to sense that this truck could carry her puppy from her, and she didn't want that to happen. So, she decided she would go also. Taking one final look at us, she hopped quickly into the truck, went directly to her puppy and lay beside it.

We drove home with our refugees! What would we do with them now? Would the mother still be hostile toward us? Would my truck become an expensive dog house, or worse yet, a battlefield?

When we arrived home, I opened the door and invited the mother to jump out. She looked at me and back at her puppy. She wanted to get out of the truck to the safety of the outdoors, but she didn't know exactly how to accomplish it. Finally, she hopped out. I quickly picked up the puppy and brought it into the yard. I sat down with the puppy on my lap and waited to see what she would do.

Slowly she came and stood and began to nuzzle her puppy. I began to stroke her head and ears, talking softly and gently to her. Then, she looked into my eyes and did something I will never forget. She reached over to my hand and licked it . . . she kissed my hand! It was almost as if she realized what I had done for her and her single remaining puppy.

The expression in her eyes was different. The hostility was gone. She looked at me as if I had raised her from a puppy. I had gained her confidence . . . she knew I was her friend. Not only had I rescued one of God's creatures, I had hopefully taught my son a lesson about life.

That night our family went to see a movie entitled "*Places In the Heart*." It was a heartwarming story about life in America in the 1930's. It depicted again the sad story of man's inhumanity to his fellow man. In the movie, a young black man was lynched because while drunk, he had accidentally killed the sheriff. After his death, the sheriff's young widow had been wronged by the banker who sought to gain control of her mortgage. I sat beside Donnie Earl. When the hooded Ku Klux Klan appeared on the screen, he turned to me and asked me if those things had really happened. I was ashamed to tell him that it was indeed a sordid part of our history.

Then I whispered to him the lesson I hoped he had learned earlier in the day with the mother dog and her puppy . . . that some people will be inhumane to both animals and people. But other people will stand up against these acts of cruelty and defend the helpless.

No, I don't see myself as a crusader out to right all the wrongs of the world. But I do see myself as a citizen of this planet who must care about what is taking place on the earth. If we allow violence and terrorism to go unchecked, the day will come when everything we hold dear will be in jeopardy.

I grow weary of reading the paper and hearing news of people killing and maiming other people. We must find a stopping place where society rises up and refuses to accept violence as a necessary by-product of life.

Perhaps we ought to discover what has created this violent climate in our society. Have you watched TV lately? Have you taken in any of the popular movies our kids see by the thousands? Check them out. Much of the content is simply "blood and guts!" Violence has been glorified on the screen. Credibility has been granted through the assent of our society, allowing social sores to fester in the name of freedom. Where is the freedom in a society that makes the vast majority succumb to the will of a few? Sounds a great deal like a restrictive, or even repressed society to me! "Is censorship the answer?" you ask. Indeed not! I understand the first amendment. I agree that basic freedoms must be guaranteed to all, even to those with whom we disagree. But I don't place poison on the table when my children are eating. They cannot make some judgments in their immaturity. That is one reason God made parents older than children! Our task is to train our offspring until they can make their own decisions . . . decisions that will make them better citizens and this world a better place in which to live. Until proponents of a "free" society can show me a better solution, I continue to maintain that we must exercise some responsibility as inhabitants of this planet to ensure that the violent, the primitive, the base, the brutal, and the cruel shall not destroy our civilization.

Today the life of a mangy little puppy may be jeopardized by someone who is cruel and brutal. Tomorrow it may be your child's life that hangs by a slender thread of human decency. We on this planet are in the process of creating a habitation for ourselves and for those who shall inhabit it after we are gone. I often look about and wonder what we are leaving for our progeny . . . men or monsters?

13

LADONNA DISCOVERS AMERICA

– January 1986 –

Father and daughter 1969

LaDonna Louise Paulk

Father and daughter 1987

J anuary and December are special months to me. Not because Christmas occurs in one and New Year's in the other. Not even because I was married in the month of December, which I was, which did, however, lead to the reason that December and January are special months to me. They are special because they are the months my two children, LaDonna and Donnie Earl, were born.

Let's talk about January 12, 1965. On that date I was in Crawford W. Long Hospital in Atlanta, Georgia, having a baby. Well, actually, Clariece was having the baby. But I was doing most of the suffering, although she tells a different story! First, let me tell you MY side of the story!

In those days the husband of any pregnant woman was regarded by medical personnel of maternity wards as the "perpetrator of the crime"! When you arrived on the premises with the travailing mother-to-be, everyone from the security guard to the elevator operator gave you a sideways suspicious glance. They fingered you as the culprit responsible for each and every pain she was suffering! All they wanted of the expectant father-to-be was that he deposit the mother safely in their arms of refuge and depart to some other place, preferably far away. There he could await their call to return and retrieve his wife and new-born baby and pay the bill! That was his major contribution to the process!

Nowadays things are so different. The father is actually considered to be a human being. He is allowed to participate in all the rites and rituals of the blessed event, such as taking pictures and giving out progress reports to waiting friends and relatives. He is made to feel as if he were some sort of hero! However, in those days he was considered to be the conspirator, perpetrator, and defendant. All I wanted to be at the moment was a fugitive!

After Clariece and I married and before she had any babies, I told her that she was so indispensable in the work of the church that she should arrange to have her babies between services. She tried her best to cooperate! Her first labor pains began shortly after the Sunday night service ended. If the attending medical personnel would have given more attention to her and less in trying to punish me for my sordid crimes against nature, she possibly would have made it back for the Wednesday night service! As it was, she had to wait until the next Sunday.

They failed to take into consideration the fact that everytime they drove me from the labor room, all progress ceased! As long as I sat there, held her hand, reassured her that I was totally repentant and would assume the role of celibacy in the future, and furthermore reminded her that millions of women before her had successfully borne children, she went about the task of delivering her child. But when I was banished to the waiting room to wait with the mass of well-wishers that had assembled in her honor, she felt totally neglected and forsaken. Her body would go into vapor lock!

Even though this slowed her down considerably, it didn't totally stop her. And so it came to pass twenty-seven hours later that she brought forth an 8 pound, 6 ounce daughter who was wrapped in hospital clothes and laid in a warmer bed! LaDonna Louise Paulk had discovered America!

The first time I laid eyes on this little lady, I fell totally in love with her! She had black hair and blue eyes. Eventually her eyes turned a deep chocolate brown, appropriate for a child whose father is a choc-oholic! The hair remained a dark brown. When I first looked at her (through a glass I might add, for they still didn't trust me near her!) I knew she was Clariece's baby because of those tiny nostrils, small replicas of Clariece's! I wondered how she would ever be able to breathe!

I had remained at the hospital during the entire delivery ordeal. I had darted from room to room, trying to stay one step ahead of militant nurses bent on putting and keeping me in my place . . . wherever that was! I was totally fatigued. I had been in the waiting room so long that other fathers whose children had been promptly delivered would pass through and check on my progress. They gave me reports on their newborns. It seemed some had even started to school in the meantime!

I went home and fell into bed exhausted. I sank into a comatose state. It seemed as if only a couple of minutes had passed when the telephone rang. I smote the alarm clock, thinking it was the offending noise. Achieving no success, I finally regained consciousness enough to realize it was the phone. I grabbed it and growled "Hello!" into the earpiece. After repeating it several times, I realized my error and turned the receiver around.

"Guess who?" a voice chirped on the other end.

My brain was in no state to play games! I couldn't even tell them what MY name was. As my mind began to clear, several responses crossed my mind, but after all I was a minister. Frankly my dear, I didn't care who was on the other end. If they didn't know who they were, I would just as soon have them establish their identity by some other method! Just before I opened my mouth to enlighten my cheerful caller that I had been rendered immobile by a runaway Mack truck, I heard the voice add, "This is the mother of LaDonna Louise Paulk, your new daughter!"

The fog was beginning to lift. Even though there remained a few cobwebs, reality was slowly beginning to take form in my senses. I was aware enough to know that at this point it was imperative that I show some degree of concern for my new daughter and her mother. I mumbled something to the effect of questioning how she was feeling. "Great!" she replied. As a matter of fact, she informed me that she had the most energy she had felt in months! She further informed me that she felt good enough to come home and clean the whole house. At this point, I suspected they had given her too many drugs! I knew I had better get back down there before she decided she was Superwoman and attempted to skydive down to Peachtree Street!

Even though she felt great, I felt as if I had just given birth to the Dionne quintuplets! All I wanted at the moment was a little rest. But I knew I had better deal with this "delivered" woman! She told me she was hungry and wanted food . . . If I didn't come soon, she would be forced to eat hospital food, a fate worse than death!

Knowing Clariece, I knew that it was important that we start making plans this morning for LaDonna's future. She would need to talk about wedding plans with the revolving stage and the sit-down dinner for five thousand people. Jesus fed the multitudes . . . perhaps I could manage with some sardines and crackers and a lot of Divine help! And then, before we knew it, there would be grandchildren . . . Whoa! First things first! Let's get her out of diapers! Speaking of diapers, that was one of my strong suits. I believe I still hold the world's land speed record for changing a diaper, cloth variety! I did it so well that I could do it in my sleep without waking me, LaDonna or Clariece. But then, come to think of it, after Clariece delivered her children, she turned them over to me for care and keeping between the hours of midnight and 8 a.m. After Clariece goes to sleep, we become a single parent family!

Once I decided to let Clariece try to put a diaper on LaDonna. When LaDonna stood up, the diaper promptly fell around her ankles! Not discouraged, she decided she would try again, and this time, tighten it up a little.

I found LaDonna walking around in a stooped position, apparently unable to walk upright. I fell on my face and began to intercede for her healing. I did what the Bible said and laid hands upon her . . . only to find the diaper pinned on so tightly and in a contortion that prevented the child from walking straight! I removed it immediately and continued my prayer of thanksgiving!

Then I realized that if LaDonna were to survive past the age of two, I would have to intervene and provide some hands-on "mothering"! Thus, I became a "co-mother."

Please don't misunderstand. Clariece is the greatest woman in the world. She is the most talented woman I have ever known. She is a gorgeous woman. She is a literal genius. But if you have ever lived with a gorgeous genius, you have discovered they have a few eccentricities . . . they deal with the weightier issues of life—like doing Christmas shopping in July and planning dinner parties for 53 live guests in a facility designed for only 12! Mundane functions like changing diapers, making formulas and driving cars are not allowed in their union!

Once LaDonna was sick and required overnight

hospitalization. We went to another hospital this time. I had been barred for life from C.W.L. Hospital because I was still considered to be the criminal element! I think they still have a lookout posted for me!

When regulation visiting hours were over, a nurse informed me that I, the father, would have to leave. Only Clariece, the mother could stay overnight. In a well-modulated voice I informed her that she didn't understand. I WAS the mother! She gave me one of those same glances I recognized from other encounters with medical personnel. She eyed me up and down to determine if a sex change operation had been performed at some time in my history. Ascertaining that a sex change was not the case, she proceeded to tell me in her own well-modulated voice that I was not very funny. If I didn't vacate the premises pronto, she would call security! I don't abide threats very well. I challenged her to bring on the gendarmes. Wanting to avert a bloodbath, she then threatened to pull down my trousers and give me an injection!

Well, that did it! I may be crazy, but I'm no fool. You can't beat a nurse wielding a six inch needle! I felt discretion the better part of valor on this day and I left, vowing to pick up the fight another day—to establish my true identity to this bastion of rectitude!

Well, LaDonna survived this ordeal and grew as a

"first" child. We always have to practice on them! Through the years I have watched her grow into a beautiful young woman. I often recall those special moments we spent together . . . watching her get the braces off her teeth, having her ears pierced, making high school cheerleader, spending sleepless nights listening to her friends chatter and giggle all night during "slumber" parties. Why do they call them "slumber" parties? I never caught anyone slumbering yet!

I have walked through many heartaches with her. Each time she cries, my heart cries with her. I still love it when she comes in, sits on my lap like she did when she was a little girl, hugs my neck, kisses my cheek and tells me she loves me. We don't want to let our little girls grow up . . . but they do anyway. Now when she leaves the house, I don't ask her where her mittens are . . . I ask whether she has her driver's license with her! But the intent is still the same . . . I have to take care of my little girl! I know the old story about no boy ever being good enough to marry your daughter. I also know that saying is not true. Somewhere, God has that man who will become THE man in her life. He will take my place as the most important man in her life. I understand that. That is the way it should be.

LaDonna is old enough to make her own deci-

sions now. Hopefully, we have trained her in the way
she should go, and when she is old, she won't depart
from those truths. But I guess I am still a part of the
old school who believes in arranging marriages. So, I
am taking applications for a husband! I have devised
a screening process that was developed at Paris
Island, S.C., Marine Training Center, M.I.T. and
Candler School of Theology. So, if you think you
have what it takes, young man, you can apply
between the hours of nine and five at . . .

14

CHRISTMAS MEMORIES
– December 1986 –

December is a month of mixed feelings for me . . . joy, but also sadness. It is a fact that there are more suicides committed in the month of December than any other month. It's not hard to figure out the reasons.

I have a pleasant memory associated with December. I was married on December 16, 1960. Another pleasant memory . . . my second child, Donnie Earl was born December 6, 1972.

And also, when we think of December, most of us automatically think of Christmas. Ah, the Christmas holidays! Indeed, there are pleasant memories associated with the season. How I looked forward to them as a child. Just think! I could get out of school a week or so before Christmas not to return until after New Year's! Plus, there were always Christmas gifts to look forward to.

Music always plays an important role in the Christmas atmosphere. As a child, I recall hearing those familiar Christmas carols as they began to reappear on the radio sometime after Thanksgiving. There were always the new jingles that came along, but I still liked the old favorites . . . *Joy, To The World, Hark! The Herald Angels Sing, O Little Town Of Bethlehem* . . . all the old faithfuls. They just "sounded" like Christmas!

When the new jingles came along, it always took a few years for them to catch on and become a part of the established Christmas repertoire. Some never made it and disappeared with the season while others took their places to be sung again year after year. I remember when *Rudolph, The Red-Nosed Reindeer* and *I Saw Mama Kissing Santa Claus* made their big hits. But still, I love to hear the familiar strains of the old carols resurrected each year.

Christmas is a time for families. We get together for meals and to exchange gifts. We catch up on all the news and make big plans to get together more during the coming year, which rarely happens! There is a special warmth and coziness in these events, especially for children. It is an important part of their "security blanket"!

But with the years, reality begins to set in and we no longer see life through the eyes of a child. We grow cynical and hardened because of the heartaches that come with life. No longer are we wide-eyed optimistic children. How sad to lose that quality . . .

I have thought of my own life and tried to see where I first began to lose the carefree attitude of a child. I recall a couple of occasions that stand out in my mind.

I was perhaps seven or eight years old when my daddy pastored a church in Greenville, South Carolina. It was a fairly large church whose members mostly worked in the cotton mills of this textile region of the south. Many of them lived in "mill villages," large communities where houses had been built by the mills for their employees. All the houses were built alike and you could find block after block of these little houses looking as if they had all been cut out by a giant cookie-cutter. The people who lived in these villages were for the most part hardworking people who kept their little frame houses very clean and neat.

These were happy villages, but as in any community, there were always the sad stories as well. I don't know why, but many of those sad stories always seemed to happen around Christmas time, which made them even more tragic.

Some of the men who worked in these mills were not only hard workers, but unfortunately, were also hard drinkers. One of these men was the husband of a lady who was a member of our church. He would physically abuse his wife and family when he got drunk. As a matter of fact, she often came to church with the knowledge that when she returned home he would physically beat her. This treatment occurred regularly. She grew weary of this and decided she could no longer tolerate his beatings. One night he returned home drunk, beat her thoroughly and then collapsed on a bed in a drunken stupor. She went out behind the house to the woodpile and picked up the ax that was used to split the wood that was used to heat the little mill village house and returned to where he lay. With one swift swing she buried the ax in his head. No longer would he beat her and the children.

The phone at the parsonage where we lived rang and a frightened voice said to my dad, "Preacher, I have just killed my husband. Would you please call the sheriff and come over here?"

I so vividly recall attending his funeral at Tom McAfee Funeral Parlor. His wife was allowed to attend the funeral services with her five little children. I recall looking into her eyes and seeing how expressionless they were. There was absolutely no emotion to be seen in her face. She stared straight ahead throughout the proceedings without shedding so much as one tear.

I followed the little group of "mourners" as it wound its way through the tombstones to an open grave on a cold, grey December day, just a few days before Christmas. The children shuddered in the cold wind as they stared at their father's grey felt casket. Some of the younger ones didn't fully realize what had happened. I remember wondering what kind of Christmas they would have . . .

This is a memory indelibly etched in my mind. To this day, when Christmas time comes, I recall the sight of those little children huddling together as they stood shivering by that open grave. Alongside their mother stood a uniformed officer who would return her to the Greenville County Jail immediately after the interment. Along with many pleasant recollections, this is also a Christmas remembrance for me . . .

There were several mill villages in Greenville . . . Mills Mill, Dunean, Judson, Woodside, Monagan and others. I recall another sad story that occurred near Christmas.

My dad and older brother, Earl Jr., were driving through Dunean Mill village when they saw people running toward one of the little mill village houses.

Daddy stopped the car to see if he could render assistance. As pastor of one of the largest churches in Greenville, and the largest congregation located within a mill village, most of the people knew him and considered him to be their "preacher," whether they attended his church regularly or not.

When they saw Daddy, they ran to him telling him they had heard shots ringing out from inside the house. They were afraid to go in. Daddy opened the door and stepped inside. There on the floor lay a little boy lying on the floor, shot dead with a wound in his head. He had fallen out of his little rocking chair wearing only one sock with a new pair of shoes beside his little body. His mother lay mortally wounded in the doorway leading to the kitchen. To the left lay a father dying from a self-inflicted wound.

No one really ever knew all the details, but from what they sketched together from others, the mother had bought a new pair of shoes for the little boy for Christmas. Somehow an argument had ensued as the child sat trying them on for the first time. The father pulled a gun and shot the lad, turned and shot his wife running through the door and then turned the gun on himself, taking his own life. Even as a child, I began to realize that Christmas was not always filled with happiness for everyone.

One of my favorite things to do as a child was to

go "window shopping" before Christmas in downtown Greenville with my parents. I recall watching
the faces of tattered little urchins pressing their noses
against the cold show windows, sadly looking at
Christmas toys they knew would never be theirs.

I recall discovering some toys at our house one
time just before Christmas and thinking they were for
me. When I didn't receive them Christmas day, I
asked about them. I remember my parents explaining
to me what an orphan was. Our church sponsored an
orphanage and the toys had been bought for a little
boy who had no parents. Even though this may
sound sad, I am grateful for those experiences. They
served to make me more grateful and more sensitive
to the needs and feelings of others.

Occasionally I grow weary of the ministry. I suppose most ministers do at one time or the other.
When I do, there are several reasons I am brought
back to my calling, and these childhood memories are
an important part of those reasons. I see those who
suffer and are heartbroken. The world races along,
catering to its own selfish desires. I ask myself, "Who
will care for those who have no one else?" The
answer always is, the Church.

Jesus Himself said we would always have "the
poor" with us. And He didn't mean just those who
were financially impoverished. He was referring to

those who were lonely and heartbroken and sick.

Then He gave examples of how we can respond to the needs of others. He told of a man who fell among thieves who attacked him, robbed him and left him for dead. Some supposedly religious people came by and bypassed him, rationalizing that either it was none of their business or they were too busy. A man of another race and religious background came along and helped him and saved his life.

On another occasion a mob of vigilantes dragged a harlot before Christ and demanded she be stoned according to the law. Jesus looked about and saw men holding stones who had made it necessary for her to turn to prostitution in order to make a living and others who had even benefited from her favors. He suggested that anyone who stood guiltless and without sin cast the first stone. The stones dropped one by one and the crowd silently dispersed.

Well, Christmas is here again. We will bring out the decorations and hoist the trees and sing the carols. We will give and receive gifts and stuff ourselves with food we really don't need. We will pass by some of those who find this season depressing. They have lost their joy in life. How will we respond to them? Will we make their Christmas season brighter?

Oh, we may sit around and tell our children about that Holy Night when the Babe was born, a

beautiful scene. But will we remember the signifi-
cance of that birth?

God saw a world that was filled with people who
were lonely, sad and sick. He saw people who had
allowed their own excesses to ruin them. He saw
children who would be disappointed because they
could not have the same joys they saw other children
experiencing. And the heart of God was sad.

It is only when our sadness is translated into
compassion that we can bring solutions. God is love
. . . and one of the components of love is compassion, a compassion that caused Him to send His Son
to heal the broken-hearted, set free the captive, heal
the sick and bring sight to the blind. And who carries
out that task today? We do . . . The Church.

No, I'm not saying "Bah, Humbug!" about
Christmas as old Ebenezer Scrooge did and discount
it altogether. But let me remind you, and myself, that
even though Christmas is supposedly a time for joy,
there are many people around us who find this the
most depressing time of the year. Many are without a
family . . . some even without friends.

If we make Christmas a time of joy for another,
haven't we given a beautiful gift? If we can make one
child smile, wouldn't that add to the joy of our holiday? If we can enhance the quality of life for a fellow
human being who otherwise would be destitute,

haven't we shared a divine gift?

And remember, it's not just the material things that bring happiness. The greatest gift we can give is the gift of love . . . wrapped up in flesh . . . our flesh. It could be the very gift that may save a life.

I give you my love. Merry Christmas . . .

15

THE SMALL JOYS OF LIFE

– October 1981 –

Clariece Miller Paulk   LaDonna

Donnie Earl

Donnie Earl and LaDonna 1987

What are the small joys of life? They are often those occasional, unexpected occurrences which bring respite from all the demanding cares of life that drag us down. In many ways, these miniscule encounters provide the impetus that keep us going from day to day . . . gifts of remembrances to savor in those moments when we desperately need a diversion in our minds. In our lives which are often plagued by hurt and pain, despair and grief, broken relationships, disappointments and tragedies they bring back the very will to live. Here are a few small joys in my life . . .

A morning smile and wave from the school crossing guard at the corner . . . Beads of sweat on Donnie Earl's nose even in the coldest winter . . . LaDonna's smile that literally fills the darkest room with dancing sunlight . . . Clariece's soft, dark eyes that without spoken words say, "We will work it out. It'll be alright."

Three stray dogs that have adopted our home as their home, and wait in the driveway with tails a'waggin' to welcome me, bathing my hand with wet tongues . . . Ginger, wagging her tail in unfeigned love . . . Lady, trying to outrun my car to the house . . . Bruno, protecting his adopted home . . .

The smell of honeysuckle . . . the two cardinals that cavort just outside my window . . . that crazy woodpecker finally abandoning his frantic pecking on my galvanized gutters at 6 a.m. . . . The sausage biscuit Clariece brings into my office in the morning . . .

Watching Donnie Earl play ball . . . watching LaDonna walk (a carbon copy of her mother!) . . . the softness of Clariece's hands . . . a rainbow . . . the sun filtering through clouds sending shafts of incandescence to the earth like gossamer streamers . . .

Childhood memories immortalizing those splendid days of yesteryear when you didn't have to worry because Daddy had all the answers . . . Psalm 91:5 when I am paralyzed with terror in the middle of a nightmare . . .

A gentle kiss from someone you know really loves you . . . a note written in a child's scribble that says, "I love you, Daddy."

Deliverance from wearing neckties . . . A chocolate bar . . . a hug from someone dear returning from a trip . . . Olivia Newton-John singing "I Honestly Love You" . . . A card with a cyclops creature bearing the caption, "I only have eye for you" . . .

A private midnight piano recital by Clariece playing "Clare de Lune" . . . LaDonna's wrinkled nose when she giggles . . . little Donnie Earl telling me an off-color joke he has heard and not realizing it is off-color . . . Clariece telling me she loves me without me saying it to her first . . . a gentle touch . . .

Glowing embers in a campfire . . . a walk in a green meadow beside a wandering crystal stream . . . a full moon against a blackened night.

Life is a collage of these kinds of memories. They are evoked unexpectedly by a sound, an aroma, a taste, a word . . . . They are precious and should be tucked away and enjoyed again and again.

May God grant us the capacity to abandon unpleasant memories and reserve only the pleasant ones . . . the memories that are lovely, the memories that are of good report . . . the small joys that mean so much in life . . .

16

JOAN...
MORE THAN A MEMORY
– June 1985 –

Joannie 1948

Joan Paulk Harris

Joan

Memories are very important to me. Some I have stored away which I take out occasionally to savor, reliving them as if they are vintage home movies I have threaded onto the old projector to run again and again. I have memorized every movement of the characters from watching them so often. Yet, I sit transfixed, as though seeing them for the first time. Some "movie memories" come complete with sound . . . but one is silent . . . each frame moving in slow motion, freezing each movement into its own eternal moment.

One such memory indelibly etched in my mind is that of a little five-year-old, blonde-haired girl with deep dimples. I see her sitting on a curb at 107 Elm Street in the sleepy southern town of Greenville, S.C. It is a hot summer afternoon. The neighborhood children have all been running and playing. Their faces are flushed with sweat running down their temples.

Suddenly in the distance from the next street, they hear the sound of a bell. Its tinkling alerts the children. The ice cream truck is on its way, making its regular summer afternoon rounds of the neighborhood to dispense Popsicles to delight the hot, thirsty children. They stop from their play, darting in different directions to beg dimes from parents or older brothers and sisters.

This little girl has garnered her dime. She sits on the curb with eyes gleaming in expectation of seeing the truck round the corner. Her name is Joan. She is my baby sister.

The last child born is usually a very special person to the rest of the family. Because of the attention he receives, often he becomes "spoiled." Perhaps because the parents have mellowed throughout the years, they relax the rules and regulations established with the first children who came along. Perhaps they are just too tired to enforce their rules. Or could it be that they have grown older and wiser? They have learned that along with the rod of correction, great virtue comes with patience, long-suffering . . . and even forgiveness for an erring child!

Even though Joan was the baby, she would not accept being "spoiled." As Christians, we often talk about people possessing a "servant spirit." If ever I saw a person with such a spirit, Joan was a demonstration of it. Before she could reach the sink or an ironing board, "Joannie" would push up a chair to wash dishes or try to iron clothes. Most little girls do this, but the desire usually fades with adolescence. "Helping" never faded in Joan. Perhaps she was born with this "servant spirit."

I think she was also born with maternal instincts. Little girls naturally play with their dolls and "mother" them, but nurturing was more than a game with Joan. It seemed to be her life! She naturally made other peoples' lives easier. It was almost unbelievable to watch her, a small girl, lugging around other children almost as old and as big as she, caring for them lovingly.

Many qualities in Joan set her apart from the ordinary . . . indeed from the day of her birth she was a "chosen" child. As I look back now, it almost seems as if her life was providentially ordered for specific purposes. She came into this world almost as an afterthought . . . but the impact she left on those of us who knew her would be life-changing!

By the time Joan was twelve years old, the other four children in our family had already married and left home. Only Joan and I remained. I was five years older than she. As she became a teenager, the years between us seemed to grow closer. During her high school years and my college years, I was the older brother who looked out for her. I personally checked out all her boyfriends! On more than one occasion, I explained things more clearly to some "ardent" young men!

I have four sisters, each holding a special place in my heart. My oldest sister, Myrtle, was like another mother to me. Ernestine, a little older than I, was my teacher. My twin sister, Darlene, was my soul mate. (I like to refer to her as my "womb-mate!") And finally there was the baby, Joan. She was my heart!

I have seen families that "played favorites." How unfortunate! I could never understand favoring one over another, for I loved all of my sisters the same . . . though each played a different role in my life. However, I felt a special "protectiveness" over Joan as the older brother still at home.

I watched Joan grow from being a beautiful young girl into a beautiful woman. Her suitors were many. I put either my "seal of approval" on each boyfriend or explained to her why I felt certain ones were not suitable! She married a young man I had come to know well in college. I knew a woman was never more prepared to make a man a good wife than Joan.

Not only was she a good wife, but in time she became the mother of a son and a daughter. She continued being the excellent mother she had proven herself to be years earlier!

She and her husband moved to Atlanta where he could work and she could be near her two brothers and attend our church. She was not just a casual member . . . she was a cornerstone of the church. She had the knack of making people feel as if they had known her all their lives. She never met a stranger . . . or a person she didn't like or who didn't like her. She became not only a tower of strength to the church, but also she became a personal intercessor for us, her two brothers. She was always sensitive to what was happening with us. Just by looking at us she knew when we were troubled. She always had the ability to say the right thing at the right time. She came through all the lean and small years with us . . . without her, I'm not sure we would have made it!

And then one day the dreaded news came. Joan had cancer! I had lost grandparents, cousins, uncles, aunts . . . but never had anyone in my immediate family faced imminent death. We were in shock! When the initial shock wore off, we realized that we must live, and if necessary, die by the same gospel we preached to others.

For three years she fought a gallant fight. At

times we thought she had it licked. It would recede into remission, only to break out in other places. At the times it seemed she had conquered it, we all rejoiced. But when it reappeared, our hearts sank again. Each time that same, old, sick feeling I had experienced when I first heard she had cancer returned.

And then on Pentecost Sunday night, just about the time our church service had concluded, Joan slipped away. An important era in my own life came to an end! The church had lost a pillar. Our family had lost its first immediate member. Donnie had lost a wife. Dana and Deanna had lost a mother. To say my loss was greater than others is unfair . . . but I know I lost someone in my life who could never be replaced. Yet because of her life, my living is richer for having had her with me those forty-one years she lived.

Now that Joan is gone, I wonder if I'll ever stop waking up in the middle of the night with an overpowering sense of loneliness. I try to close out those things that bring back the pain of her loss. Yet occasionally I find myself seeking them out . . . little reminders . . . like driving by the house she and her family built to enjoy. Another family enjoys it now. I look at her pictures . . . I see her handwriting on little notes. I can't forget her . . . I don't want to forget her!

I miss her . . . I miss her laugh. It was one of those infectious laughs! When she laughed it made everyone around her want to laugh. She loved to be happy and tried desperately to bring happiness and joy to everyone around.

Joan was a natural-born peacemaker. She hated to see conflict among others and would go to whatever lengths necessary to restore peace and tranquility. Jesus said "Blessed are the peacemakers for they shall be called the children of God." Indeed, she was a daughter of God, created in His image and bearing His character in her life . . . and in her death! I recall during her last hours bending near her ear to whisper, "Joan, you are a daughter of the King!" The trace of a smile crossed her lips.

I miss her smile . . . even when she was in pain, that beautiful smile was often still there. It said more than words. It reassured us that even though the body was growing weaker, her spirit was growing stronger. It was as if while her natural sight grew dim, she began to focus more clearly on a heavenly vision. Remember how Stephen saw the image of Christ when he was dying? Even so, in those moments she seemed to see things the natural eye could not see, comprehend, or explain.

Indeed, on Easter Sunday afternoon, she saw an

image of Christ. Later she related how He came to her bedside and comforted her. We sensed details that she dared not tell us about that divine visitation . . . after all, we still see through mortal eyes. From that day forward, her spirit seemed to be of another world. She had caught a glimpse of eternal things. The things of this earth seemed to "grow strangely dim in the light of His glory and grace."

I miss her touch. She had beautiful hands . . . so delicate, feminine and soft. I so vividly recall those times when just a squeeze of her hand communicated so much love and understanding.

I miss her voice. I recall the early days of our church when she was THE soprano section of the choir. Her voice could always be clearly distinguished above all the others . . . clear as the bell of an ice cream truck on a warm summer afternoon . . .

Even though Joan is dead, she still lives on among us in many ways. Not only does she live in the memories we have of her, but she lives on in the lives of her children . . . both are blessed with so many of her characteristics. Her son Dana and her daughter Deanna have moved in with my family. You see, they are more like a brother and a sister to LaDonna and Donnie Earl than cousins.

At times I watch them and see a great many things about them that are so typically Joan. It is a joy to have them close to me. For as long as they live, the spirit of their mother lives on!

I enjoy writing letters to people I love, for I have always felt perhaps I could communicate better in writing than any other way. And so, I write a letter to Joan . . .

Dear Joan,

You know that I still cry a lot because I miss you so much. I try not to let people see me cry or know the reason I am crying. Isn't that silly? Why can't we cry openly about things that are so dear to us? This is probably the hardest column I have ever written. I have to stop often and wait until I can see the letters through the tears again!

You must know how much I miss you. But I wouldn't bring you back if you had to suffer again. I admit I am still mortal and think in finite terms. But I so long to see you . . .

Shortly after you left, Deanna graduated from high school. When she walked into my office wearing her cap and gown, humming "Pomp and Circumstance," I thought I would go to pieces. I had to fight back the tears . . . she wanted you here for her graduation so badly! You would be so proud of your kids, Joan. I have never seen anyone as brave.

I still cry when I see your name plate on your

office door. We just don't want to take it down. It isn't there to keep us from forgetting you . . . it's as though as long as it's still there, perhaps one day you may just walk back in, having only stepped out for a moment.

Joan, I often wondered why the scene of your sit-ting on the curb in Greenville comes to my mind so often. Finally, I remembered the rest of that story. One day Mama told you not to go outside. I don't recall why . . . perhaps you were sick or were being punished. But you were standing at the screen door when you heard the ice cream truck bell. You ran to me and asked for a dime. I don't even remember where I got the dime or why I had it, but I gave it to you. I'm not even sure I was aware you weren't supposed to go outdoors. I do remember that I felt guilty because you were outside when Mama spotted you on the curb.

She called you in before the truck got to the house. You were crying, partly because the ice cream truck wasn't there yet and partly because you realized that you were in trouble! I recall the feelings of sym-pathy I felt for you . . . just a little girl crying for an ice cream on a sultry, summer day.

I begged Mama to let me take the spanking for you. I told her I had given you the dime, and therefore I was to blame for your being outside. I was not a "martyr" by nature. It was quite out of character for me to volunteer for pain . . . but something about the look of expectancy on your face that day caused me to want to do whatever possible to keep you from being disappointed.

I think so often of that look on your face. I see that same look on your children's faces occasionally. I have the same desire to do whatever necessary to keep them from being sad. I know we can't take your place, but we are so glad they are a part of our home now. They are no longer children . . . they have become mature adults, living by the principles they were taught as small children.

I wish I could ask you questions about heaven. I understand we are unable to see clearly through that "dark glass." I do sense your "presence" so often. On Sunday I look down where you always sat. I am occasionally overcome with human grief when I realize you are gone . . . and I cry. Thankfully, I am in church and people can still cry in church services without attracting a lot of attention!

But then I realize that you are there! I recall the scriptures that tell of the "cloud of witnesses" that surround us. In my imagination, I see you gathered with the others who have gone on. I can almost hear the conversations you carry on about us! Most of all, I feel you "pulling for me." I feel sometimes as if we are on the field of battle. All of you are standing in the viewers' gallery, shouting encouragement to all of us. And when

I sense that, it gives me a reason to fight even harder to be victorious.

Joan, I know you understand I still have human frailties and make so many mistakes. Please understand them. I miss you so much . . . Did I tell you how much I loved you when I had you with me? Did I help take any burdens from you? If I failed you, please forgive me. Thank you for what you left me . . . the memory of your life and love. I do look forward to being with you again . . . I love you . . .

Love, Don

Perhaps it took losing someone so dear to me for me to have a clearer understanding and perspective on life. Through Joan's death, hopefully I can better comprehend how I should live today. May I learn my lesson well for the sake of the Kingdom of God . . . for heaven's sake!

Mail this card for FREE one-year subscription to *Thy Kingdom Come* monthly newspaper.

Please send me:

☐ FREE one-year subscription to *Thy Kingdom Come* monthly newspaper.

☐ A book and tape catalog of messages by Earl Paulk.

☐ Please put my name & address on the mailing list for Earl Paulk Ministries.

Name _____

Address _____

City _____ State _____ Zip _____

Telephone (_____) _____

How did you receive this book?   ☐ Bookstore   ☐ Friend   ☐ Direct Mail   ☐ Television Ministry